The Many Faces
of Bereavement

The Nature and Treatment of Natural, Traumatic, and Stigmatized Grief

The Many Faces of Bereavement

===

The Nature and Treatment of Natural, Traumatic, and Stigmatized Grief

Ginny Sprang, Ph.D.
and
John McNeil, D.S.W.

BRUNNER/MAZEL
A member of the Taylor & Francis Group

Library of Congress Cataloging-in-Publication Data

Sprang, Ginny.
  The many faces of bereavement : the nature and treatment of natural, traumatic,
and stigmatized grief / Ginny Sprang and John McNeil.
      p.   cm.
  Includes bibliographical references and index.
  ISBN 0-87630-756-X
  1. Bereavement—Psychological aspects. 2. Grief. 3. Death—Psychological
aspects. 4. Sudden death—Psychological aspects.
I. McNeil, John S. II. Title.
BF575.G7S67   1995
155.9'37—dc20   95-16267
                                                                          CIP

Published by
Brunner/Mazel
A member of the Taylor & Francis Group
325 Chestnut Street
Philadelphia, PA 19106

Manufactured in the United States of America
10 9 8 7 6 5 4

Contents

Introduction

Death and dying have been a concern of mankind as long as humans have existed. Evidence of this concern is the increased value that has been placed on life as civilization has evolved and the multiple ways survivors have developed to deal with the loss of loved ones. Special attention has been given throughout history to the death of significant figures, but until the past two or three decades little attention has been given to the possibility that there may be variability in the manner in which individuals respond to the death of a loved one.

Within this more recent time span, there have been numerous attempts to achieve theoretical and conceptual clarity regarding the symptomatology, process, and duration of grief. Kübler-Ross (1969) described the process of bereavement in terms of stages of grief. Worden (1982) criticized this conceptualization, arguing that stages of grief may be taken too literally so that symptom deviation from this model runs the risk of being viewed as dysfunctional, when in fact the symptoms may be very adaptive. Worden contends further that the stages of grief as presented by Kübler-Ross (1969), Doyle (1980), and others imply passivity, thereby adding to feelings of helplessness and loss of control. To support his contentions, Worden developed the "Tasks of Mourning" as a way of empowering the mourner to take an active role in grief recovery.

Other researchers, such as Zisook and Devaul (1984), have developed psychometric measures of grief that include acute mourning and unresolved grief as separate but highly related concepts. These theoretical and conceptual ambiguities impede empirical development in the study of bereavement, as well as limiting the delivery of services to grieving individuals. In addition, representatives of special populations are especially impaired as uncertainty prevails regarding what responses can be expected and what factors influence the extent of the reaction.

These theoretical debates among traditional grief theorists are further complicated by the lack of conceptual clarity regarding the distinction between normal and pathological grieving in the *Diagnostic and Statistical Manual of Mental Disorders*, Fourth Edition (American Psychiatric Association, 1994), which fails to take into account variables such as the mode of death. Historically, our understanding of grief has been seen as a reflection of the times, encompassing societal expectations and standards, community practices, and the normative factors relating to and causing death. With the industrialization of society, the variables contributing to how individuals die have changed, and thus, so has the process of grief. Today, with the increase in violent crime, advances in technology, and the transformation of values and standards, we see an increase in murder, drunk driving fatalities, community disasters, and the type of illnesses (e.g., AIDS) that threaten human life.

Just as the manner in which humans live and die has changed, so must our conceptualization of "normal" mourning behavior change as well. To apply traditional models of grief across all populations, irrespective of the manner of dying, is injudicious and limits the clinician's ability to appropriately assess and intervene. Though many theorists have noted the significance of the mode of death variable in determining grief outcomes, evaluation of this variable has historically been done in anecdotal form, and there is little empirical literature proposing typologies of grief based upon the nature of the death.

While it is the contention of this book that the mode of death is a significant and often overlooked variable in the conceptualization of grief, one cannot lose sight of the valuable contribution made by the traditional conceptualizations and operationalizations of bereavement and its elements. Therefore, this book will explore the development and specifications of traditional models of grief to underline the importance of what is known about the process of grief, considering variables such as relationship, age, and personal characteristics of the mourner, as well as providing a framework of symptomatology specific to nontraumatizing, nonstigmatizing deaths for the purposes of comparative and theoretical specification. It is proposed that what is known about the grief response following the death of a spouse, a child, or an aged parent has valuable implications for grief model development considering other modes of death such as murder, drunk driving, AIDS, critical incidents, and suicide, though these conceptualizations are insufficient in explaining or predicting outcomes with these other types of grief.

The book is organized into three sections. The first provides an overview of traditional models of grief. Sections II and III cover suggested typologies of grief specific to the mode of death for traumatized and stigmatized grief processes, respectively. Treatment implications for each of these three sections are presented as an outgrowth of this study. The treatment chapter in Section I provides a general summation of treatment strategies and considerations, as a resource to the therapist as well as a point of comparison for future discussions on intervention. The treatment approaches in Sections II and III are largely based upon the personal experience of the authors as well as on contributions from the literature.

It is hoped this book can be used as a clinician's resource for understanding and treating the many dimensions of grief experienced in society today. By further development and expansion of the current body of knowledge concerning the way individuals grieve, it is the authors' desire to point clinicians and researchers in the direction of intervention and policy development that may attenuate the negative effects of death and dying among the many misunderstood survivor-victims and "secret survivors" currently suffering in isolation.

I

DEATH BY NATURAL CAUSES

1

A Theoretical Overview of Traditional Models of Grief

The discussion of death is one of the most avoided topics of conversation in society. Despite a flood of material that has been produced concerning death and dying and the resulting effects on the survivors, there is still considerable ambiguity regarding the factors that impact the nature, course, and duration of the grief process.

The majority of the literature on the bereavement process concerns the psychophysiological reactions of the mourners following a death from natural causes, illness, or accidents. Traditionally, the process of grief has been understood relative to attributes such as: (a) relationship of the bereaved to the deceased; (b) age of the deceased; and (c) personal characteristics of the survivors. Historically, grief theorists have appeared to recognize the mode of death as an important consideration in the conceptualization of bereavement. However, their examination of the mode of death variable has been preliminary, at best. This book proposes that the mode of death is a significant but often overlooked dimension in the determination of grief responses. In addition, it explores the considerable variation relevant to the specific characteristics of the loss. The purpose of this exploration is twofold: (a) to explain the importance of the abovementioned variables on the nature and course of subsequent bereavement, and (b) to provide a framework of symptomatology espoused by traditional models of grief for the purposes of comparison with traumatic and stigmatized models of grief and to further delineate the specific theoretical tenets.

To adequately understand the impact of death on the survivors and the affective, behavioral, cognitive, and physiological manifestations associated with the death, the meaning of attachment must be explored.

Bowlby's (1973) attachment theory provides a conceptual framework for understanding this phenomenon. An individual's need for security precipitates the formation of strong emotional bonds and is indicative of the basic human tendency to survive. Bowlby's thesis that security and safety are primary motivators for the development of attachments is supported by the observation of similar behaviors in animals. In his writings, Bowlby describes young children and young animals who during the development process periodically leave their primary attachment figure to explore their environment, always returning for support and reassurance. The disappearance of the attachment figure induces intense anxiety and distress. Bowlby (1973) goes on to state:

> If it is the goal of attachment behavior to maintain an affectional bond, situations that endanger this bond give rise to certain very specific reactions. The greater the potential for loss, the more intense these reactions and the more varied. In such circumstances, all the most powerful forms of attachment behavior are activated— clinging, crying, and perhaps angry cohesion . . . when these actions are successful, the bond is restored. If the danger is not removed, withdrawal, apathy, and despair will then ensue. (p. 42)

Lorenz (1963) describes this grief-like response in the separation of the greylag goose from its mate in the following example:

> The first response to the disappearance of the partner consists of anxious attempts to find him again. The goose moves about restlessly by day and night, flying great distances and visiting places were the partner might be found, uttering all the time the penetrating trisyllabic long distance call. . . . The searching expeditions are extended farther and farther . . . and quite often the searcher itself gets lost. (p. 40)

All of the objective, observable characteristics of the anxiety manifestations in the separated child and in the greylag goose roughly parallel the human bereavement process. Bowlby (1973) suggests that there are significant biological forces that influence the response to separation and are expressed in an automatic, instinctive way with aggressive behavior. The responses of animals to separation demonstrate that biological processes may influence the loss of attachment response in humans, yet there are features of this response that are unique to humans. These reactions are conceptualized as the bereavement process.

DEFINING THE NOMENCLATURE

An essential element in understanding the various dimensions of the bereavement paradigm explored in the following chapters is an accordance of interpretation of the terminology used to describe the concepts.

The term *bereavement* is a model used to explain the emotional state that results from the loss of a loved one. The expression of suffering is defined within a cultural context and is influenced by a number of variables, which will be explored throughout this book.

Grief is an associated concept that generally refers to the emotional components of the bereavement process. The essence of the grief response is often multidimensional, reflecting not only the loss of a loved one, but also the loss of identity and purpose.

Mourning is the behavioral component of bereavement and is most influenced by sociocultural influence and expectation.

The *process of grief* is understood in terms of a progression through a series of tasks or stages. Ochberg (1988) describes these tasks as:

> the expression of affect, the understanding of the meaning of the lost person or object, the elucidation of ambivalence in the relationship, and the eventual freedom to attach trust and love to new significant others and, in appropriate ways, to new replacement objects. (p. 10)

Engle's (1961) thesis parallels the death of a loved one with the experience of being severely wounded or burned. He states that the grieving process represents the loss of well-being and requires a psychological healing similar to the physiological healing necessary to recover from a physical trauma. Engle believed the terms *healthy* and *pathological* or *abnormal* applied to various courses grief may take in the psychophysiological process. This approach is similar to the tenets of developmental theory, which claim that there are certain developmental tasks that must be completed as a child grows. If the child fails to complete a task on a certain level, adaptation is impaired when the child is trying to complete tasks at a higher level. Engle (1961) applies this theory to the grieving process when he postulates that the failure to complete grief tasks or stages can impair future growth, development, adaptation, and resolution.

Uncomplicated grief has been conceptualized by Zisook and Devaul (1984) as "a painful, but self-limited reaction to loss which more or less follows an overlapping sequence of phases with a brief period of shock and denial, merging into a phase of dysphoria and ending in a sense of resolution" (p. 169). DSM-IV states:

> The bereaved individual typically regards the depressed mood as "normal," although he or she may seek professional help for relief of such associated symptoms as insomnia or anorexia. A diagnosis of major depressive disorder is generally not given unless the symptoms are still present two months after the loss. Certain symptoms are not characteristic of "normal" grief reaction: (1) guilt about things other than actions taken or not taken by the survivor at the time of death; (2) thoughts of death other than the survivor feeling that he or she would be better off dead or should have died with the deceased person; (3) morbid preoccupation with worthlessness; (4) marked psychomotor retardation; (5) prolonged and marked functional impairment; and (6) hallucinatory experiences other than that he or she hears the voice of and transiently sees the image of the deceased (pp. 684–685).

Although there are factors other than the mode of death that are predictive of complicated versus uncomplicated grief, normative grief processes tend to be less complicated than traumatic or stigmatized bereavement episodes.

STAGES OF GRIEF

Kübler-Ross (1969), Doyle (1980), and Westberg (1971) have identified phases or stages of normal grief to explain the process of grief and to provide clinicians with a framework for identifying problems. It should be noted that a bereaved person may experience more than one stage at a time and does not necessarily experience symptomatology in the order presented here. Many of the stages outlined by these authors have commonalities. For purposes of this book, the following stages of grief will be offered as a comprehensive representation of the "stage models" of grief.

STAGE ONE: Attempts to Limit Awareness: Shock, Denial, and Isolation

Shock and denial protect the mourner from experiencing the total extent of the reality all at once. Denial is usually a temporary defense, eventually replaced with at least partial acceptance that a death has occurred. Accompanying the denial and shock is social isolation as the mourner may engage in self-protective actions to ward off others who may trigger overwhelming emotional states.

Historically, the grief process was facilitated by supporting family members and friends, religious rituals, social traditions, and customs. Today, the bereaved person must often face the struggle with grief alone. Neighbors often do not know what to say and choose to avoid the mourner. Families may be separated geographically and may be present only for the funeral.

The isolation and withdrawal of social resources can be linked to the urbanization of society that has caused the destruction of many traditional communities and rituals associated with death and dying. In the absence of some of these supporting structures, some individuals may not effectively deal with the tasks of grieving. Therefore, adequate social resources are important to facilitate appropriate passage of the mourner from one stage of grief to another. Shock and denial are considered healthy responses after a death by natural causes as long as these reactions do not extend for more than a few days (Doyle, 1980; Kübler-Ross, 1969; Westberg, 1971). Gardiner and Pritchard (1977) cited six extreme examples that illustrate prolonged and extreme forms of denial. The individuals involved in their study exhibited manifestly psychotic, eccentric, and reclusive behavior (e. g., keeping the body of the deceased in the house for a number of days prior to notifying anyone of the death) in an attempt to deny the loss.

STAGE TWO: Awareness and Emotional Release

As the shock and denial begin to diminish, the mourner may experience the second stage of grief—emotional release. As the individual affectively acknowledges the death, feelings of anger, guilt, and resentment, along with physiological symptoms of distress, become evident. Anger generally results from the frustration over the loss of control or the inability to change the situation. Anger can be expressed toward medical personnel, the self, the deceased, or other family members.

Guilt is often a common theme at this point. The closer the bereaved's relationship with the deceased, the greater the possibility for feelings of guilt to surface. Family members may assume culpability for the death and may feel their actions may have in some way caused the death or failed to prevent it. Guilt is most evident in the responses of parents after the death of a child. Society's orientation to children is one of supporting them and helping them grow to their full potential. Parents have been entrusted with the task of providing life and protecting children from harm. Latour (1983) postulates that parents can be extremely angry and guilt-ridden, perceiving the death as personal failure. Role theory can be utilized to explain this phenomenon. Davis (1986) states that "social identity is the sense of ourselves that we derive from the positions we occupy and the adequacy with which we and significant others judge our role in society" (p. 546). This theory implies that our sense of self-identity is damaged by a perceived failure to adequately fulfill the role expectation dictated by society.

Kübler-Ross (1969) describes the concept of bargaining, which often occurs at this time in response to the overwhelming feelings of anger and guilt. Bargaining is usually witnessed in the early phases of the grief response when the mourner has not come to terms with the finality of the death. The mourner may attempt to make a deal with God by promising change in beliefs or behavior if the death can be reversed.

The emotional responses experienced during this phase of the grieving process are necessary for healthy adaptation to the loss (Zisook & Devaul, 1984). Often, there are gender differences that impact the affective acknowledgment of the death. Rando (1984) states that society tends to discourage emotional responses, especially in men, though it is a normal and essential part of grieving for most individuals. Withholding emotional responses can be unhealthy and lead to abnormal grief reactions. Davidson (1979) cites many cases of physical symptomatology in bereaved individuals that could not be traced to organic etiology. He concludes that individuals who do not allow themselves to grieve may develop medical symptoms and a deterioration of physical health. He theorizes that pain can be a symbol for suppressed grief.

The most common symptoms of physical distress are appetite and sleep disturbances, headaches, nausea, and gastrointestinal difficulties. Anxiety disorder symptomatology may be present due to feelings of panic associated with overwhelming affect, leading mourners to believe they are going crazy. This panic state may be induced by the psychological disorientation and disorganization of the grief response, or the fear that the emotions or their intensity is abnormal.

STAGE THREE: Depression

Depression ensues when denial of the loss can no longer be maintained and attempts at bargaining have failed. Depression manifests when the mourner views the situation as hopeless. Discomfort at the affective acknowledgment of anger may cause grieving individuals to internalize the angry feelings, due to a need to regulate their affect and/ or an absence of coping skills to deal with the anger and guilt. Depression after a loss is a normal reaction, though a prolonged reaction (over two months) suggests a complication by a Major Depressive Episode in the DSM-IV (APA, 1994). However, what constitutes a prolonged duration is not clearly defined.

Wolfelt (1988) provides possible distinctions between depressive grief and other forms of depression. In a normative grief response, the individual is responsive to offerings of support and comfort, whereas depressives may be unwilling to accept support. The bereaved individual is openly angry and can relate symptoms of depression to a specific aspect of the loss (i.e., the inability to say goodbye) as opposed to the depressed individual who does not overtly display anger but is irritable and expresses generalized depression symptomatology. In normal grief, individuals are able at some point to experience moments of happiness, whereas a depressed individual is not.

There is also a distinction in the affective presentation of the individual: grieving individuals present as acutely sad and empty, whereas depressives project an ongoing sense of hopelessness and helplessness and display a chronic emptiness. There are also differences in the chronicity of physical symptoms of distress.

STAGE FOUR: Acceptance and Resolution

In the final stage the individual "comes to terms with reality." There is a reinvestment in social activities, and the individual is able to talk about the loss and remember the deceased without experiencing severe emotional upheaval. The mourner begins to feel hopeful for the future and becomes involved in new activities and relationships.

CRITICISMS OF THE STAGE MODELS OF GRIEF

The "stage models" of grief have been challenged by researchers who believe that the models may not address individual idiosyncrasies and other variables that may impact passage through the stages of grief. From a methodological standpoint, there are obvious limitations. The research on these stage models has relied on clinical observation of small, nonrepresentative samples (Bowman, 1980; Burgess, 1975; Doyle, 1980; Poussaint, 1984). Generally, comparison groups have not been included.

Although there is general agreement regarding the symptomatology of grief reactions across the models of grief espoused, the conceptualization of the process has been called into question. Worden (1982) criticized the stage models of grief, stating that individuals do not always progress through the grieving process in an orderly fashion and may experience more than one stage at a time. He argues that clinicians and clients may take the "stages of grief" too literally and may inappropriately judge deviations from this model of grieving as dysfunctional.

The Tasks of Mourning

Worden (1982) addresses this issue by developing the "tasks of mourning," thereby supplementing previous descriptions of the grief process with specific mourning behavior. He believes that the stages of grief imply passivity, something that the individual must endure helplessly. Tasks, on the other hand, are more congruent with the concept of grief work by implying that the grieving individual has power over progression through the grieving process. They also imply that the grieving process can be influenced by intervention, thus providing hope to the mourner. This model has the most implication for intervention and does not vary greatly in its description of the symptomatology of grief.

Duration of the Grief Response

Another criticism of the stage models of grief is that they fail to provide a temporal framework for understanding the duration of the grief response (Silver & Wortman, 1980). Indeed, there have been conflicting data regarding the length of time necessary to successfully complete the process of grief. Davidson's (1979) survey of individuals who had *not* experienced the death of a significant other found that the majority of these respondents expected the grief response to be completed within two weeks. Bornstein and Clayton (1972) conducted multiple interviews between one and 13 months with 109 widows and widowers following the death of their spouse and concluded that only 17% of their sample were definitely or probably experiencing symptoms of grief at the final interview, and most were better within four to six months of the loss. Parkes and Weiss (1983) refute these findings, based on their longitudinal study of bereaved individuals who were interviewed two to four months following the loss. Over 40% of the sample were rated by trained interviewers as showing moderate to severe anxiety at that time.

The lack of empirical definity regarding the duration of the grief response is most likely based on the number of endogenous variables (i.e., personality) influencing the individual's response to loss. Factors such as the relationship between the bereaved and the deceased, the abruptness of the death, the mode of death, cultural influences, and other external factors must be explored further.

THE ANTICIPATORY GRIEF FACTOR

Certain types of death provide for the mourners a pre-death grief process, which may impact the nature, course, and duration of the bereavement process. Death of the elderly and deaths due to terminal illness may include an anticipatory or forewarning period in which the survivors may begin the process of grief prior to the loss of life. This phenomenon was first observed by Lindemann (1944) when he noticed the absence of overt symptoms of grief in survivors who reported to have experienced many of the stages of grief prior to the death of their loved ones. The "anticipatory grief" process has been examined by many researchers (Aldrich, 1963; Kübler-Ross, 1969) since Lindemann's observation in 1944. Although it is clinically important for practitioners who work with patients and families prior to an anticipated death to have a good understanding of the anticipatory grief process, empirical evidence of the impact of this process on post-death bereavement is equivocal in nature. Exactly how this anticipatory phase impacts the course of bereavement will be examined in the following chapters.

CONCLUSION

This section has focused on describing the most traditional understanding of the bereavement process, based upon Bowlby's theory of attachment and loss. It provides a framework of symptomatology that focuses on variables such as the relationship of the bereaved to the deceased, the age of the deceased, and personal characteristics of the survivors. Essential to successful completion of this task is the exploration of how these models were developed and their significance to current perceptions of normal mourning behavior. Specifically, the grief response following the death of an elderly person versus the grief response following the death of a child will be discussed in the following two chapters. It is hoped the foregoing review of traditional models of grief will serve as a point of comparison for the subsequent analysis of grief relative to the mode of death.

2

The Grief Response Following Spousal Death, with an Emphasis on the Elderly

Our traditional understanding of grief has been based in many ways upon anecdotal and empirical evaluation of the grief response following the death of the elderly. By definition, this raises the issue of natural versus unnatural death and how society dictates bereavement behavior. The following discussion will examine these issues historically, as well as the multiple causal variables that impact the nature, course, and duration of the grief response.

Grief responses following death are determined largely by the societal attitudes and beliefs regarding death. These views about death have changed over time. Various writers have emphasized different determinants—for example, secularization of death and its de-ritualization (Kamerman, 1988), and cultural factors and life expectancy rates (Kastenbaum & Aisenberg, 1976). Some attention to these trends and shifts seem crucial to any discussion of bereavement.

Throughout history, death has been an ever present reality with which the living have had to contend. Medieval history is filled with records of thousands of deaths resulting from catastrophic plagues caused primarily by unsanitary living conditions. The bubonic plague of the 14th century is estimated to have killed one-fourth of the earth's population (Kastenbaum & Aisenberg, 1976). Most persons did not live to reach a "ripe old age" or to realize the biblical promise of fourscore and ten years of life expectancy. In the United States, life expectancy in 1900 was 47 years, in contrast to approximately 75 years in 1990. Life expectancy from birth was low because of high death rates from acute infectious diseases, and maternal, infant, and childhood deaths.

Today, people are more likely to die from chronic diseases or accidents. Kamerman (1988) has observed that at the turn of the century an individual could not pass through childhood without experiencing the deaths of several members of the family, whether old, young, or middle-aged. As a result, death was a common occurrence and could not be hidden from public view as is the practice today. Current life expectancies, however, have shifted death from an event that happens over the life span to one that is perceived to happen to old people. Coupled with the lack of exposure to death is its attachment to a low status group in our society, the elderly.

Paralleling these trends have been changes in the philosophical meanings attached to death. Primary among these changes has been a shift from a sacred to a secular view of death (Kamerman, 1988). Biblical teachings had espoused a continuum of conception, birth, life, death, and afterlife. Life, then, is a natural progression in which death does not represent finality, but instead movement on to a better place where the streets are paved with gold, there is perpetual peace and contentment, there is happy reunion with past loved ones. From a sacred perspective, death is not to be feared, but rather to be sought after following a life of trials and tribulations. Secularization, in contrast, has led to avoidance and denial of the actuality of death.

Lack of belief in the religious promise of an afterlife brings one face-to-face with the finality of death, thereby making it too traumatic to deal with directly. Society has been kind enough to create multiple avenues of avoidance. Dying no longer occurs at home, but in institutions. In 1949 slightly less than half of deaths in America took place in institutions, but by 1958 this number had risen to almost 61%, and in 1982 it was 68% (Kamerman, 1988). In New York City, the proportions were even higher. Death has been professionalized. Institutional death, in effect, means that it is handled by the health professional: physician, nurse, and hospital chaplain. Even if family members are present, they may not be allowed in the room of the dying person at the point that death occurs. Preparation of the body for burial likewise is not handled by the family but by another professional, the Funeral Director. Avoidance is easy and convenient; in fact, it is expected, and the nonconforming are discouraged.

Denial is facilitated through our focus upon a youth-oriented society. The myth that death happens only to the elderly allows its eventuality to be denied by those younger. Kamerman (1988) has suggested that even the body preparation is indicative of the denial. A Funeral Director receives positive platitudes to the extent that the dead body looks as the person looked while still alive. We don't feel comfortable talking to the bereaved about death. To the dying person we talk as if death were not imminent. Euphemisms abound as ways of saying that someone has died (e.g., going to a better place, passed on, God needed another flower in his garden).

Patterns of mourning attest further to the denial attempt. There has been a move away from the wearing of traditional mourning clothing. The black color conveyed the message of bereavement. This badge of sorrow gave permission to the bereaved to mourn and also dictated the behavior of the observer. Roles were fairly clearly established for both. The mourner was comforted in the act of showing proper respect for the deceased. For the observer, these role prescriptions are crucial because people generally experience discomfort in the presence of the recently bereaved. Prolonged wearing of mourning clothing is not acceptable, and the traditional bouquet of flowers hung on the front door to denote the death of an occupant is no longer seen. Survivors are encouraged to hasten the period of mourning and get on with their lives.

These changing and contradictory trends and messages have made a very difficult task even more difficult for the elderly bereaved. The elderly have already been removed from the mainstream of society, devalued, and relegated to low status. There is high likelihood that they were not present when the person they are grieving for died. Few guidelines are available to direct "proper" bereavement. In view of these problems, one is forced to ask, What is the pattern of bereavement of the elderly survivor? To answer this question one must also deal with the issue of natural versus unnatural death.

Thus far, it has been argued that society has depicted death as something that is reserved for old people. In industrialized societies, when a child, young adult, or middle-aged person dies, the death is considered premature or out of the natural sequence of things. The death of a child, for example, has received considerable attention (see Chapter 3). *Natural death*, which is at best an elusive term, is a death that occurs in the normal sequence of events. An elderly person dies, naturally, as a consequence of the aging process following the laws of nature. A death may be considered unnatural if it occurs to a younger person and was caused by something outside of the normal progression of the course of life. Included here would be such things as accidental deaths, suicide, or homicide.

This definitional description becomes quite problematical when younger individuals die from illnesses before they reach the promised biblical 70 years. Kastenbaum and Aisenberg (1976) have suggested that natural death is one that has not been tainted by human hands. Here they seem to be speaking to homicide and suicide. Continuing, they suggest that society needs a concept such as natural death because it serves a palliative purpose for the following reasons:

1. The death of an old person may strike us as natural in that we are not taken by surprise.
2. There is nothing else that we might have done or should have done.
3. Death of an elder is natural in that it bolsters our faith in the natural order. (pp. 376–377)

Although the term *natural death* seems to escape precise definition, it is generally taken to mean that death is natural if it happens to an elderly person, but is unnatural if it happens to a young person. When death occurs to an older person, however sudden, it is to be expected; therefore, it should mitigate the grieving process for the survivor. This position, however, minimizes the importance of the intensity of emotional attachments that may have developed over the years.

The concept of natural death, though, necessitates exploration of its definitional implications. Even in the most ideal of situations, *natural* is an elusive term. Merriam-Webster's Collegiate Thesaurus (1976) offers several definitions, but the general definition is "common, commonplace, matter of course, normal, prevalent, regular, typic, typical, usual." This definition is interesting and instructive in that it focuses upon a routinized course of action or process. When the adjective *natural* is used to modify death, some unsettling dissonance is created. Death, across all cultures, has never been treated as a routine matter, but rather as something that requires enormous societal energy and ingenuity to either deal with it directly or to create mechanisms for minimizing or avoiding the power of its impact.

Historically, it was impossible to escape dealing with death on a fairly frequent basis due to a limited life expectancy. It was literally unreasonable to think that one could reach adulthood without having been touched by the death of many of those one knew. Numerous ritualistic procedures were prescribed that regulated the behaviors of the survivors. Avoidance was not one of the behaviors. Moreover, adherence to a religious creed helped soften the trauma of the loss. Within the last century, much of this has changed markedly. Scientific advances, improved technology, and a reordering of societal priorities (especially in Western cultures), have made it easier, and undoubtedly more convenient, to relegate death and grieving to a subordinate position in our society. To some extent, this seems to work for a majority of the population—or does it? If the answer to this question is No, then as a society we have not arrived at a point where death can be seen and accepted as a natural event. Even if death itself is perceived as natural, surviving significant others have probably not been able to conceptualize grief and mourning in the same way.

Considerable literature exists to indicate that multiple variables operate as determinants of the course and intensity of bereavement following the death of a significant other, including the elderly. The following section will identify and discuss a number of these variables and how they impact survivors of the deceased, even if the death is considered to be a natural one.

FACTORS AFFECTING BEREAVEMENT FOLLOWING SPOUSAL DEATH, WITH SPECIAL EMPHASIS ON THE ELDERLY

Acceptance of an event as a natural process should conceivably lessen the devastating impact following its occurrence. Death, as has been pointed out above, may or may not be accepted as a natural process, but this is in part influenced by the age of the deceased. The older the person at the time of death, the more likely it will be seen as being natural. Several studies reported in the edited book *Older Bereaved Spouses* (Lund, 1989) suggest that the overall impact of bereavement on the mental and physical health of surviving spouses, in fact, may not be as devastating as one is prone to suspect. These findings, however, should be considered with caution as they are based upon self-reports regarding perceived health and life satisfaction and measures of depression. Distinguishing where grief ends and depression begins is at best a difficult and controversial task.

Lund (1989) summarizes the findings of nine studies undertaken in four geographic areas of the country:

1. Bereavement adjustments are multidimensional, in that every aspect of a person's life can be affected by the loss. This includes physical and mental parameters, as well as external stressors such as financial factors.
2. Bereavement is a highly stressful process, but many older surviving spouses are quite resilient. Most agreed that the death was the most distressing experience they had ever dealt with, but their coping strategies held them in good stead.

3. The overall impact of bereavement on the physical and mental health of many older spouses is not as devastating as expected.
4. Older bereaved spouses commonly experience simultaneously both positive and negative feelings. (This finding is certainly consistent with theories regarding the stages of grief. It supports the belief that death often engenders ambivalent feelings.)
5. Loneliness and problems associated with the tasks of daily living are two of the most common and difficult adjustments for older bereaved spouses. For many, loneliness persists well into the second decade following the loss. Tasks of daily living impact one's independence and may be reflective of the level of physical and mental well-being.
6. The course of spousal bereavement in later life might be best described as a process that is most difficult in the first several months but improves gradually, if unsteadily, over time (the improvement may last for many years or, for some, the bereavement may never end).
7. There is a great deal of diversity in how older bereaved adults adjust to the death of a spouse. (pp. 218–221)

Two vignettes illustrate this diversity:

> Mrs. V is a 64-year-old widow whose husband died approximately five years ago. Initially, Mrs. V felt overwhelmed and wondered how she could exist, much less function. For several months, she floundered, relying heavily upon support from her two adult children and from friends. Eventually, she forced herself to begin managing the rental property that she and her husband had accumulated, feeling that failure to do so would be an insult to his efforts to ensure a secure retirement for both of them. At the same time, Mrs. V began attending the local senior citizen center and participating in their activities. Subsequently, she enrolled in continuing education courses structured for retired persons at the local university. This educational experience prompted Mrs. V to apply for admission to a graduate school of social work. Mrs. V's married daughter with two children returned to school also and now at the age of 38 is about to graduate from medical school. Mrs. V beams with pride when telling of how she and her daughter decided that anything is possible, in spite of hurdles, if one makes a committed decision to persevere.

> Mrs. S, a 59-year-old widow, was admitted to a private psychiatric hospital following a suicidal gesture in which she ingested 8

milligrams of Valium, four Vicodin, and several ounces of alcohol. This behavior occurred on the fourth anniversary of her husband's death. Mrs. S lives alone and is supported by a small annuity that accrued from her husband's death and by earnings from a job as an insurance clerk. She has family in the local area, but has little contact with them, including her four children.

Mrs. S has a lengthy psychiatric history, with several hospitalizations over the past few years. She has been chronically depressed and treated with psychotherapy and Desyrel, plus medication for hypertension. Mrs. S's emotional condition has not improved significantly since the death of her husband. She feels that her job performance is satisfactory and that occasionally she derives enjoyment from attending movies and from dancing. She is considered at high risk for recidivism due to past psychiatric history, lack of social support, and failure to follow through with treatment recommendations.

These findings are indicative of the highly complex and multifaceted nature of grief and mourning. Considering these factors, a logical conclusion is that different empirical studies will show conflicting results. This is, in fact, proven true as the literature is reviewed and analyzed. Numerous contradictions exist when demographic variables such as age, gender, income, educational level, and marital status are examined. Similar contradictions are apparent relative to affective, behavioral, and perception variables such as social supports and their utilization, sense of well-being, self-esteem, and self-efficacy. The effect of some of these variables will be examined.

Spousal Relationship

One of the causal variables affecting grief following the death of a spouse is that of the relationships of the bereaved with the deceased. Holmes and Rahe (1967) reported over 25 years ago that death of a spouse was the most severe stressful event that an individual could experience. Their study was not specific to an elderly population, but perhaps it is more poignant in view of the fact the older bereaved spouse has fewer opportunities to replace this significant loss, and the relationship is likely to have existed for many years. Relationship, however, cannot be seen in isolation from its importance to the surviving person. In fact, it has been suggested that the first variable in bereavement is the degree of importance the deceased had in the life of the survivor (Hickey & Szabo, 1973, cited in Sinick, 1977). The fact that the couple may have been married for a number of years does not necessarily indicate the degree of importance that each had for the other. Dershimer (1990) emphasizes the quality of the lost relationship. He suggests that the more emotionally involved a relationship was the more severe the bereavement (p. 30).

Additionally, the extent of dependency on the deceased person bears a direct relationship to the bereavement process. Dependency includes emotional as well as material aspects. Even if the marriage has been less than perfect, bonds were developed and social interactions or exchanges were fostered that structured the parameters of the relationship. Role expectations were consciously or unconsciously evolved. Death of one of the role players creates a vacuum that must be filled during the bereavement process if pathological adaptation is to be avoided.

Sanders (1989) has reported the differences between older and younger bereaved spouses. She found that younger bereaved spouses initially showed greater shock, confusion, personal death anxiety, and guilt, coupled with feelings of disbelief (p. 181). This would seem to support the ideas around the natural versus unnatural death dichotomy. The case of Mary dramatically demonstrates this type of response.

> Mary was 26 years of age when her husband was killed in a motor-cycle accident, leaving her with a one-year-old daughter. At the time of the death, they were separated, at Mary's insistence, because of her husband's drinking, abusive behavior, and suspected infidelity. The evening of the accident, he was reported to have been driving at an excessive speed prior to losing control of the motorcycle and careening into a stone embankment. When informed of the accident and death by the police, Mary collapsed and did not fully regain awareness until after her arrival in the emergency room of the local hospital. Crying uncontrollably, she could not believe her husband was dead and became increasingly distraught when informed of the details of the accident.
>
> As the reality of the death became inescapable, Mary blamed herself and felt guilty about making him move out of the home. Over the next several days, she became very depressed, but managed, with familial support, to get through the funeral planning. She struggled to avoid acting on intrusive suicidal thoughts because her daughter needed her.
>
> Mary was referred to a mental health clinic where she received grief counseling. For almost a month, she was able to function only marginally, at best. During the second month her depression lifted somewhat and she began to do an adequate job of caring for herself

and her daughter. At the end of three months she had returned to work and decided to use the husband's insurance benefits to buy a home for herself and her daughter. Treatment was terminated.

Older bereaved spouses, in contrast, seemed to use denial to diminish the grief reaction. Denial, however, appeared as "determined optimism." Maintaining this optimistic outlook was difficult as the older bereaved realized that time was at a premium, physical health was tenuous, and being alone raised concerns about personal safety and deprivation (Sanders, 1989).

Relationship, both the quality and the nature of it, is obviously a critical variable affecting the bereaved spouse. Consideration of the impact of relationship exceeds the legal definition of marriage, but perhaps more importantly the quality of that relationship. Another relationship that has garnered attention is that of the bereaved adult child who experiences the death of a parent.

THE DEATH OF THE PARENT OF ADULT CHILDREN

Empirical research regarding the impact on adult children of the death of a parent has been limited. More typically, researchers have targeted reaction to the death of a spouse or parental reaction to the death of a child. Of the studies that have been reported, most conclude that the response of an adult child to the death of a parent is less severe than that of the loss of a child or a spouse (Osterweis, Solomon, & Green, 1984; Owen, Fulton, & Markusen, 1982; Sanders, 1989).

In the Owen et al. study (1982), the authors conclude emphatically that when bereavement patterns are compared among spouses, parents, and adult children, the adult sons and daughters reported the fewest adjustment problems. Several differences were noted among adult children: smallest increase in the use of tranquilizers, less anger, less preoccupation with memories of the dead parent, fewer physical complaints reported, and the least sense of feeling punished by the death. Sanders (1989) similarly noted that "where three types of death were studied (child, spouse, parent) it was found that the death of a parent showed the lowest level of grief intensities." She observed that adult children usually redirected their attachments to others, such as their spouse or children.

There are undoubtedly multiple factors influencing this outcome. Among the other reasons for the grief response is that adult children have other life tasks that may take precedence, such as marital relationships, career goals, parent-adolescent conflicts, and reassessment of self. Parental loss, for an adult child, is, therefore, less important when placed against other life tasks than if it had been the death of a younger person.

Owen et al. (1982) indicate that the age of the child and parent also may be causal variables. A younger surviving child is likely responding to the death of a younger parent, so the parent-child bonds may be much stronger. They also report the bereavement response more nearly mirrors a normal grief reaction if the death was that of a cross-sex parent. The grief is less intense, in other words, if it was a daughter-father or son-mother combination.

In contrast to the findings that parental death of an adult child is less disruptive than in the case of a spouse or child, Douglas (1990) believes the death of a parent may be one of the most critical events in adult development because of the great probability that the relationship with the parent may have been, for many, their most enduring relationship. In addition, such a death brings to the fore one's own mortality. In the normal course of life, the elderly die first, so when a parent dies the adult child is next in line, the buffer is gone. Horowitz et al. (1984), in a clinical study of persons seeking psychiatric treatment following the death of a parent, concur with Douglas and concluded that the surviving adult child suffered a "measurable degree of symptomatic distress."

The idea of life tasks and their prioritization seems critical, as reflected in the following vignette.

> Mrs. A, a 65-year-old married mother of one child, experienced the death of her own centenarian mother five years ago. Although geographically separated for years, the family unit of eight children remained extremely close as a nuclear family. The father had died 20 years earlier. Almost daily there was telephonic contact with one or more family members so that everyone was always current on family matters. Mrs. A was a central figure in the communication network and influential in not allowing the filial reverence and responsibility to deteriorate. She had been very close to her mother (and deceased father). In fact, after completing her professional education and securing employment, she built a "family home" for her parents, where they resided until their respective deaths. When the mother died, there was considerable concern about how Mrs. A would handle the loss.
>
> Prior to the death of her mother, Mrs. A's only child, a young adult, was diagnosed with a severe, progressively deteriorating illness. While she grieved the death of her mother, a central priority was attending to the needs of the adult unmarried child's efforts

to embark on an academic course that would facilitate his coping and decrease the likelihood of later becoming reliant upon public welfare resources.

Other life tasks clearly preempted grieving over the mother's death and the family feared maladaptive grief response.

Although the research evidence generally posits the idea that the death of an elderly parent of an adult is less devastating than other types of death, the possibility exists that many persons may be suffering in silence. Society tends to be impatient with prolonged bereavement and perhaps even more so if it happens to be the death of the elderly parent of an adult child, because, after all, the old are expected to die.

GENDER

Much of the research regarding gender differences relative to the bereaved has focused upon younger age groups, with attention specific to the elderly being more prominent within the past two decades. Although findings about gender differences are at times ambiguous and contradictory, there does seem to be some degree of consistency that males and females grieve differently. These differences are perhaps more striking among younger bereaved persons. For example, girls (child and adolescent) long for "comforting and reassurance, leading to sexualized relationships," whereas boys engage in antisocial behavior such as petty theft, car stealing, fights, drug usage, and challenging authority (Osterweis et al., 1984, p. 113). Men are less likely to experience a loss of sexual yearning and, in fact, expect new partners to accept their grieving for the lost mate. Women, in contrast, could not engage in new relationships, feeling that it would be disloyal to the deceased (Osterweis et al., 1984, p. 73). Without controlling for age, Sprang (1991) has summarized the findings of various researchers. Her research of the literature found that there is a heavy emphasis on cultural and societal factors.

When gender differences are examined specifically relative to elderly persons, there is substantial agreement. In fact, Lund, Caserta, and Dimond (1989) concluded in their study that there is more similarity than difference in the manner that both genders grieve. Their study reported on 192 bereaved persons who were asked to complete questionnaires six times during the first two years of bereavement. The first data collection was three to four weeks following the death.

One finding, however, that consistently seems to distinguish men from women is that widowers are at greater risk for adverse health outcome than widows. Several studies report a significantly increased mortality rate for elderly widowers during the first six months to a year following the death of their spouses. This outcome was decreased markedly if the widower remarried (Osterweis et al., 1984, pp. 20–25).

Conventional social roles also play a part in coping strategies used by the elderly that differ somewhat relative to gender. Satisfactory resolution of the bereavement process necessitates successfully making role changes. Golan sums this up succinctly as it applies to females. She suggests a process of change that involves moving from being wife to widow to woman (Osterweis et al., 1984, p. 74). Role changes of both males and females are inclined toward learning new skills that were antithetical to their roles in the marriage. Widows learn skills traditionally reserved for men, such as minor house repair or managing business aspects. Widowers develop competencies in such things as meal preparation, laundry, and shopping (Lund, 1989, pp. 137–138). Remarriage rates for elderly men are expected to be greater because the opportunity for remarriage is better for elderly men since women outlive men, making the potential marriage pool of men smaller. Men and women will experience some aspects of bereavement differently, but when global indicators are considered, such as loss-related feelings, mental and physical health, and social life, they have more in common than they have differences.

RELIGIOUS BELIEFS

Religion is generally accepted as being a powerful force in the life experience of most people. Although it may wax and wane throughout the life cycle, religious conviction guides the behavior of individuals and is a source of strength to be called upon in times of need or crisis. In spite of the widespread acceptance of the importance of religion in our society, there is some difference of opinion regarding its impact upon the bereavement process. As a consequence, religious beliefs may be seen as a help or hindrance in the attempt to deal with the grief process.

Some believe individuals who are religiously oriented are probably better able to accept and cope with death than nonreligious persons. For those who believe in an afterlife, death poses only a limited separation from the deceased and eventually loved ones will be reunited. Belief in a higher power outside of one's self can serve as a source of comfort to the survivor. Turning to God provides a sense of belonging, which in turn appears to positively affect well-being (Wuthrow, Christiano, & Kuslowski, 1980). There appears to be some consistent agreement that women seem to turn to religion during the grieving process more frequently than do men (Sprang, McNeil, & Wright, 1989).

Lund (1989) analyzed the results of over a dozen studies regarding the bereavement of older spouses, in which he was involved directly or peripherally, and concluded that "the present research evidence on older spouses shows that religion-related variables have not explained much of the diversity in long-term bereavement adjustments" (p. 33). Religious participation and religiosity, however, did seem to have some beneficial effect upon psychosocial adjustment. Religiosity was not defined, but religious participation was defined as "keeping busy" with religious tasks.

Religion can also have a negative impact in certain types of situations. The person may experience a crisis in faith, which questions why God let the deceased die. Religion alone may be helpful, but is probably most beneficial when it is buffered by strong family interaction. Negative consequences could also ensue in some individuals who believe in an afterlife because the deceased could be watching their behavior and making positive or negative judgments about it (Caserta, Van Pelt, & Lund, 1989).

While many of the studies cited above included survivors of all age levels, they do point out the differential nature of religion upon the grief experience. The studies dealing specifically with the elderly indicate that religion, when taken alone, at best has limited effect upon the bereavement process. Although religion may be an important factor, bereaved persons need other people, which calls attention to the critical value of a social support system.

SOCIAL SUPPORT

If one accepts the admonition that "man is not an island," then the importance of social support becomes abundantly clear. There appears to be considerable consensus regarding the need for social support during the period of bereavement, but the degree of agreement declines when one questions effectiveness relative to factors such as quantity, quality, and the time that support is provided. Historically, bereavement has been facilitated by supporting family members and friends, religious rituals, social traditions, and customs. Societal changes, among other things, have probably increased the likelihood that supports may not be available when they are needed.

Stroebe and Stroebe (1987, as cited in Sanders, 1989) have observed that there are three different types of support that may be provided to the bereaved. They are:

1. Instrumental. Functions related to the funeral, advice on financial matters, help with personal or household tasks. This type of support is needed first.
2. Emotional. Here, the essential task is that of encouraging grief work. This involves being empathic and helping the bereaved accept the reality of the death.
3. Validational. The bereaved need to know that the grief process is normal and that they are not going crazy. (Sanders, 1989, p. 219)

Timing of the help is crucial. Support provided at the time of death greatly influences subsequent adjustment to the death of the spouse (Schuster & Butler, 1989). In contrast to this finding, Parkes and Weiss (1983) concluded that the "presence of supporting relationships, while valuable at the time of bereavement, had no significant association with later recovery. What did seem important was not whether support was initially available, but whether it was available and utilized." This latter comment is important because it is not uncommon for the bereaved to isolate themselves and not use available services. Caregivers may therefore need to reach out assertively, but gently and empathically, to the bereaved.

CONCLUSION

As this chapter points out, the death of the elderly has been seen as a natural death. Our understanding of the grief process is generally based upon bereavement as expressed by aged widows and widowers. Spousal death occurs at younger ages also and may impact individuals differentially. Society considers death of the older person as following the laws of nature and dictates mourning behavior accordingly. Unfortunately, this premise has influenced expectations about the process of grief across populations regardless of the mode of death or other significant variables.

In contrast, the death of a child violates the laws of nature and is viewed generally as unnatural. The suddenness or unexpected nature of the death confounds traditional conceptualizations of bereavement. The following chapter on parental grief will explicate these variations.

3

Parental Grief

There is widespread agreement that the death of a child is one of the most difficult losses that individuals experience. Osterweis, Solomon, and Green (1984) write that any bereavement is painful, but that the experience of losing a child is by far the worst. Supporting this same position is Sanders (1989), who concludes that the death of a child is an "unbearable sorrow," a wound that "cuts deeply, ulcerates, and festers. Scar tissue is slow to form. For some it never heals." The amputation metaphor is sometimes used to describe the loss of a child as much like the amputation of a limb (Klass, 1988). If the limb that is lost is a leg, the individual learns to walk again, but the healed stump is always there as a reminder.

Considerable inconsistency exists regarding many aspects of bereavement, but this is not the case when dealing with the loss of a child through death. Little variation in the impact is found regardless of the manner in which the death occurred. Various writers, however, offer slightly different reasons for the intensity of the grief response. These discussions rely heavily upon the dynamics of the parent–child relationship.

PARENT-CHILD RELATIONSHIP

All living animals develop their phylogenetic manner of relating to their offspring. With lower order animals, the primary concern may be simply to place their eggs in the least threatened environment; after that the offspring are on their own. Higher order creatures assume varying degrees of responsibility for nurture and protection beyond the point of birth, in contrast to the sea turtle, which lays its eggs in the sand and

26

leaves the hatched young one to fend on its own. One thing that is held in common by all, however, is concern about the future. Creatures at the lower end of the evolutionary chain are concerned primarily about the perpetuation of the species. Higher order species, in addition, evidence greater concern about physical well-being and safety needs.

Humans exhibit a complex configuration that includes physical as well as psychological needs. The child is an extension of the parent and as such represents the genealogical future of the family line and dreams, hopes, and expectations of the parents. The parent, therefore, has a unique bond with the child that is perpetuated by a myriad of interactional patterns. Bonding may begin as soon as the verification of conception and increases as the pregnancy progresses, with the mother's attachment probably intensifying earlier than the father's.

Psychoanalytic theorists would premise the parent–child relationship upon the conscious and unconscious dynamics that occur during the developmental years of the child. Both literally and figuratively, the child is an extension of the parents that assures their future. Birth of the child is living proof of the masculinity of the father and the femininity of the mother, symbolic of the sexuality of each. Parents are expected to assume the omnipotent responsibility of provider, protector, and problem solver. Should shortcomings in any of these roles occur, it represents failure on the part of the parent. Loss of the child through death indicates the ultimate failure, and some part of the parent is likewise lost since the child is an extension of the parent.

The death of a child is a shattering, unparalleled loss regardless of the circumstances of the death, age of the child, whether or not there are surviving children, or any of the other variables thought to impact the grief response. Much of the work regarding grief has relied upon the model of bereavement following the loss of a spouse. When used to evaluate parental grief, bereaved parents are likely to be viewed as grieving pathologically. Parental grief results in more somatic reactions, greater anger, guilt, depression, and despair during bereavement than among persons who are grieving the loss of a parent or spouse (Sanders, 1989). A different model is therefore needed to assess and treat parental grief. Among the writers who have proposed a model of parental grief are Sanders (1989) and Rando (1986b). Both of these will be discussed.

Sanders

Sanders reports from a 1979–1980 study of bereaved Tampa, Florida, residents who had experienced the loss of spouse, parent, or child. She proposed that there are six parental responses to bereavement: despair, confusion and conflict, guilt, anger, somatic problems, and marital problems.

1. *Despair*—Parents give the appearance of having suffered a physical blow that left no will or strength to fight because they have suffered a loss of part of self. Vulnerability is, therefore, a prominent feature. They move through an unreal world asking, Why? There is a visible raw pain.
2. *Confusion and conflict*—Pronounced confusion is obvious in the early stages of grief. Inability to concentrate is a major symptom, but there is an intent alertness about anything concerning the dead child. Indecisiveness is common, including decision making around habitual activities. Constant preoccupation with the lost child makes concentration extremely difficult, if not impossible.
3. *Guilt*—Feelings of guilt run extremely high because parents feel responsible for the child's welfare, even before birth. Expectations for the child are forward projections coupled with their role as facilitators of these goals.
4. *Anger*—This is one of the most severe reactions experienced, precipitated by the overwhelming feelings of impotence. The sense of powerlessness is a direct refutation of the earlier accepted role of protector, provider, and problem-solver. There are six types of anger: confrontive, displaced, ambivalent, internalized, helpless, and appropriate.
5. *Somatic problems*—Bereaved parents have a large number of somatic problems, which is indicative of the high degree of stress they are undergoing.
6. *Marital problems*—One estimate is that 75% to 90% of all married couples have serious problems following the death of a child. Much is related to their inability to help each other at this very critical time and to the likelihood that each is handling the grief in a different way, which may be misinterpreted by the mate. (pp. 165–171) (Disagreement with the marital conflict premise will be discussed later in this chapter.)

Rando

Rando (1993) suggests a three-phase model consisting of the avoidance phase, the confrontation phase, and the reestablishment phase. The *avoidance phase* is characterized by shock and denial, plus various emotional reactions consistent with the temperament of the parent. The *confrontation phase* encompasses the myriad of responses that occur when the parent can no longer avoid the actuality of the death of the child. Reactions such as anger, fear, guilt, anxiety, depression, and search for meaning, as well as physiological manifestations, emerge. The *reestablishment phase* arises when the intense grief decreases and the parent begins to reenter the reality of the need to continue living.

The patterns of parental grief explicated above by Sanders and Rando show considerable similarity to the traditional spousal loss model, but reveal the magnified intensity of the bereavement of surviving parents. These models reflect a number of symptoms that justify a DSM-IV diagnosis of Major Depression or, perhaps, Dysthymic Disorder.

Making the adjustment even more difficult is the fact that society has not defined a clear role for the bereaved parent. There is not even a word in the English language to identify the bereaved parent. In spousal loss, the survivor is widow or widower. Accounts abound in the literature relating to the difficulty bereaved parents have responding to seemingly routine questions. For example, if asked how many children the parent has, she may wonder if the deceased child should be included in the count. In fact, if the dead child was an only child, do the parents justify the label parent? In contrast, the public seems not to hesitate about whether to refer to a retired minister or physician as reverend or doctor. Society has not defined a clear role for the bereaved parent. It is the responsibility of the parent to create and define his own role and then adjust to that role. The door is, therefore, opened to considerable role confusion.

Role confusion needs to be differentiated from role conflict. Role confusion occurs when there is not a defined role and the individual is not sure how to behave. Role conflict, in contrast, occurs when the individual is aware of the expected role behavior, but for some reason elects not to act in accordance with that role. The bereaved parent is not conflicted, but rather is confused. Society tends not to be charitable in its appraisal of the confusion of the person who is uncertain of his or her role behavior. This provides fertile ground for symptoms such as anxiety, depression, anger, and indecisiveness.

The ambiguity created by this set of circumstances calls for a different model for the bereaved parent.

NEED FOR A DIFFERENT MODEL OF GRIEF

It has been argued persuasively that there is need for a different model of grief when one is assessing and treating bereaved parents. In the mid-1980's, Rando evaluated the adequacy of the traditional model of grief and its applicability to grieving parents (Rando, 1986b). She utilized the tasks model of grief espoused by Worden (1982) to argue the need for a different conceptualization. Worden had proposed a task model of grief, in contrast to the prevailing stage models. Students of the stage models had indicated that there was a progression of levels through which the grieving person must pass in order to successfully complete grief work. Failure to do so suggested fixation at a lower level, thus complicating the grief process. Until the bereaved had negotiated all of the stages, their grief work was not complete. This fixation could then interfere with their satisfactory social functioning. Tasks models minimized the stage process and insisted that successful grieving necessitated the completion of certain tasks to get beyond nonfunctional bereavement and subsequent movement toward getting on with one's own life. Worden (1982) identified four tasks of mourning that needed to be accomplished for the individual to recover from the bereavement process. These are:

1. Accepting the reality of the loss
2. Experiencing the pain of grief
3. Adjusting to the environment in which the deceased is missing
4. Withdrawing emotional energy and reinvesting it in another relationship (pp. 11–16)

It was proposed that each of these tasks posed special difficulty for the bereaved parent. Task one, accepting the reality of the loss, is extremely difficult, if not impossible, in that it challenges the natural order of things (parents die first) and destroys the parental myth of omnipotent protector, provider, and problem-solver. When there is more than one child, parents may invest their energy into parenting the surviving children, thus effectively denying the loss of the deceased child. If the dead child is an adult, the separation from the home most likely occurred several years previously, so the loss is not as visible, making acceptance of the reality somewhat more problematic.

Task two, that of experiencing the pain of the grief, is undoubtedly more severe than that felt in mourning other types of losses. Lack of an adequate support system additionally intensifies the pain as well as unrealistic societal expectations that are placed upon the grieving parent.

Task three, adjusting to the environment in which the deceased is missing, creates a major problem if there are surviving children in the family. There remains the necessity of parenting the other children. This, then, is markedly different from spousal loss, where role expectations with the significant other is removed completely. Death of an only child in a single-parent family is more similar to the death of a spouse, but all of the ramifications of parental grief remain. For some insight into the loss of an only child in a single-parent family, see Gillis (1986), who paints a poignant picture of the overwhelming feelings of being "alone" that engulf the single parent who has lost a child. Often, the status of single parent has been acquired as a result of death or divorce. This may lead to the parent and child seeing themselves as facing the world alone. Their lives may become so enmeshed and intertwined that they are more than simple parent and child—they are strength, support, and a confidant for each other. When this significant other half is lost, the future may appear to have been destroyed.

Task four, withdrawing emotional energy and reinvesting it in another relationship, is quite problematic because the child is literally an extension of the parent and a part of the parent. Decathecting from the child is essentially an attempt to decathect from one's self. If reinvesting energy into another relationship means having another child, society may view this as a replacement child, with all of the negativism involved in that term. It may be easier for a surviving spouse to reinvest in another relationship than it is for a parent to do likewise.

Without doubt, an area that begs for further research and theory building is that of the nature of parental grief. Rigorous research looking at causality is sorely needed. Some selected variables are already believed to be significant.

CAUSAL VARIABLES

Age of the Deceased Child

Age of the deceased child, when considered by the nonaffected general public, is probably not seen as a significant factor influencing the grief response. Nichols (1986) has spoken of "discounted grief and negated death" when death claims a child at the lower age limits of the life spectrum. She is speaking primarily of newborn death and stillbirth. The right to grieve a death is also denied to those suffering a loss because of miscarriage (Lietar, 1986). Society condemns, similarly, severe displays of grief following Sudden Infant Death Syndrome (SIDS). The message that society seems to be giving is that grief of a death is illegitimate unless the child has reached some unclearly specified age level. Since SIDS occurs typically within the first few months of life, society does not appear to condone or accept the need for severe or prolonged grief until the modal age for SIDS has passed.

Mourning rituals, similarly, do not exist for losses from miscarriage, perinatal conditions, or early life complications. In fact, in the case of early miscarriage, hospital personnel may unilaterally dispose of the "tissue" without consulting the parents. Questions may arise regarding the appropriateness of a funeral if it was a stillbirth. All too often the mother may be left out completely in the planning for the dead child, out of protective concern for her. If there is a funeral, no universally accepted guideline exists as to whether it should be private or public (Peppers & Knapp, 1980; Schiff, 1977).

These inconsistencies pose particularly difficult problems for parents grieving losses occurring from any of the above listed conditions. The loss is considered relatively insignificant since the child has never lived as a viable human being or, supposedly, it has not been around long enough to allow the development of attachment bonds. Verbal and behavioral messages convey these beliefs to the grieving parent both from professional caregivers and well-intentioned friends. Society fails to understand that attachments can be intense regardless of the age of the child, and bonding may occur during pregnancy, especially with the mother.

Deaths that occur early in the life spectrum create their special kinds of problems, but death of a child at any age is especially difficult for parents. Children, in the natural order of things, are supposed to outlive their parents. Whenever this order is reversed, it is excruciatingly painful to the surviving parent. The child represents the future; death destroys this expected pattern. Death of an adult child can be as painful to the parent as the loss of a school-age child or adolescent. To the extent that societal proscriptions or prohibitions exist, it appears that society is more charitable in the latitude it allows mourners if the age of the deceased child is somewhere midway between the continuum poles of infancy and later adulthood.

Gender

When gender is considered, it is necessary to consider the sex of both parents and also that of the deceased child. The literature reports, fairly consistently, that when parental grief is assessed, there is in fact a difference in the grieving styles of mothers and fathers. Coupled with this is the great likelihood that mothers grieve more intensely and for longer periods of time than do fathers. In a study limited by a relatively small sample size and quasi-experimental design, Fish (1986) provides some insight into parental gender differences. He administered the Grief Experience Inventory (GEI) plus another instrument developed for the study to 112 bereaved parents, 77 women and 35 men, who had been bereaved from one month to 16 years. Significant differences were found in the grief scores between mothers and fathers.

The mean GEI scores indicate marked differences in the intensity of grief experienced by mothers and fathers. There is a consistent decrease in male scores over time, whereas the scores for mothers increased after two years and decreased after five years to a level only slightly less than that scored during the first two years. Several reasons are possible for this variation, such as that mothers may feel more isolated and lack social support. Differences in male/female grieving styles have been summarized by Klass (1988). Women tend to feel the loss as isolation and are, therefore, more sensitive to parental distance. Women may grieve more publicly. Men, by contrast, grieve privately, but see the loss as a void and seek solitude.

The previously cited study by Fish (1986) is also a source of information in determining if the sex of the deceased child influences the grief response of the parents. Results reflect that fathers grieve more intently over the loss of sons than of daughters, and there was more incongruence between parents over the loss of a daughter. This difference is probably most pronounced during the first four years of bereavement.

Religion

Religion has been considered consistently as an important variable to study in the quest to understand the grief response. Invariably, when a child dies, regardless of age, parents seek to find some meaning in the death. This search for meaning turns most often toward religion. In the natural order of things, parents are supposed to die before their children; when this sequence is reversed, reasons for it are sought. The bereaved tend to look to an omnipotent, omnipresent, omniscient God for an answer. For some bereaved parents, their faith in religion is sorely tested. For others, their faith may be strengthened. The direction their faith takes is probably related to the level of satisfaction obtained in the search for meaning. Cook and Wimberly (1983, as cited in Sanders, 1989, p. 176) indicated that there are three types of religious commitment that influence bereavement outcome of surviving parents: (1) reunion with the deceased child in Heaven, (2) the child's own faith as an influence on many lives, and (3) the child's death as a punishment for wrongdoing.

Reuniting with the child in Heaven seems to blunt the finality of the loss, while simultaneously offering a reconnection in a beautiful, carefree afterlife. The idea of the child's influence on others suggests some type of altruistic purpose in the death. By dying, the child positively influenced the life of others; therefore, the goodness of the child's life is ongoing in spite of death. Guilt is the essential component that is inherent in the third factor, punishment for wrongdoing.

Martinson (1991) in a study of bereaved parents whose child had died of cancer reported that 71% of parents believed that their religious commitment positively affected their grief response. Consolation and acceptance were the predominant experiences.

Kushner (1981) in his book *When Bad Things Happen to Good People* offers a different perspective that moves away from seeking meaning in the usually described manner. Typically, parents want to know why this happened to their child. In seeking meaning within this context, the griever is placed in the position of then deciding if there is a good God or a bad God. Kushner's thesis departs radically from the idea that God makes individual decisions about everyone, as is reflected in the song, "His Eye Is on the Sparrow, So I Know He Watches Me." He suggests that God created the earth with a design of randomness and has, therefore, left things to happen on the basis of probability theory. When catastrophic or horrible things happen, God is not delivering a cruel or punitive message. Likewise, when good things happen, God has not intervened personally. This perspective seems to be particularly beneficial for individuals who cope primarily in a cognitive manner.

Religion does appear to play an important part in the grief of parents. Qualitative analyses abound in the literature that supports this conclusion (Klass, 1988; Schiff, 1977). Practice wisdom developed through clinical experience also supports this.

Marital Stability

A preponderance of evidence seems to support the idea that marital discord and/or divorce have a high likelihood of occurring following the death of a child. Without specifically stating so, it appears that this eventuality is believed most likely if the child is still a child (i.e., younger than an adult and still dependent to some degree upon the parents for support). Estimates of the frequency of the occurrence of severe marital problems range from the 75% to 90% by Schiff (1977) and Simpson (1979) to the 24% to 70% divorce rate quoted by Kaplan, Grobstein, and Smith (1976) and Strauss (1975).

Several reasons are suggested for this course of events, but all appear to resolve around two or three overlapping issues: (1) differing styles and patterns of grief, which lead to (2) spouses not being synchronized in their grief work, which results in (3) spouses nonavailability to each other during this critical time of need for support from a significant other.

Earlier in this chapter, the study of Fish (1986) was cited as showing the marked differences in grief scores between husbands and wives, with husbands seeming to grieve less intensely. This creates a built-in situation for each spouse to misperceive the grief response of the other. Further misperception can occur because each may be at a different place in handling the tasks of grief and mourning. Since both are bereaved and engrossed in their own pain and hurt, they may not be able and/or willing to give of themselves to the other. Rather than providing the needed emotional support to the mate, each may distance from the other. If the marriage was not stable prior to the death of the child, the current crisis and stress may be more than the marital bonds can endure.

In contrast to the pessimistic picture depicted above, some writers have suggested that the marriage may, in fact, be strengthened. Crisis theory certainly supports this supposition in that a crisis can be seen either as a time of danger or as a time of opportunity. The study of Lansky, Cairns, Hassanein, Wehr, and Lowman (1978) concluded that bereaved parents may have lower divorce rates than the general population. A 1981 study by Foster, O'Malley, and Koocher (1981) also rejects the premise of inevitable divorce. In fact, the crisis of the death of the child made spouses more attuned to the negative and positive aspects of the marriage. Consistent with crisis theory, the couple would then be "ripe" for positive change. Miles and Crandell (1983) found that bereaved couples saw the crisis of the death of their child as an opportunity to build a stronger relationship.

Thus far there is no unanimity regarding the impact of the death of a child upon married couples. This conclusion is supported in a Canadian study of bereaved parents who had suffered the loss of an infant. The researchers suggested that there were three different groups of couples. One group was comprised of those whose marriage was not stable enough prior to the death to survive the strain of the infant's death. A second group included those whose marriage was sufficiently strong to help each other through the bereavement. The third group was composed of those couples whose marriage will perhaps break up in the future (Lang & Gottlieb, 1991). The authors of this book concur with this categorization of three groups.

CIRCUMSTANCES OF THE DEATH

After the child has developed beyond the infancy stage, the probability of death decreases markedly. When death does occur, it is most likely to be the result of terminal illness or an accident. Other possibilities are things such as suicide or the result of acts of violence. Several studies have been done in an attempt to determine if the manner of death influences in any significant way the pattern or intensity of the grief experience of the survivors (Sanders, 1989; Sprang, 1991; Sprang, McNeil, & Wright, 1993). Findings from selected studies will be discussed below.

Terminal Illness and Anticipatory Grief

Death following a chronic and/or terminal illness, in contrast to sudden death, may be thought to be easier to cope with since the survivors have had time to prepare for the loss. Lindemann (1944), in his seminal work, thought of anticipatory grief as the progression through the phases of grief prior to the loss of the loved one. Although Lindemann indicated this process might be beneficial to the mourner as a "safeguard against the impact of a sudden death notice," he noted that the process might have adverse consequences if the grief work was done too effectively and the anticipated death did not occur.

Much of the information regarding parental grief has been gathered from studies or observations of parents struggling to deal with the death of a child from cancer. The parents' and child's efforts are depicted as they traverse through the difficult journey that begins with diagnosis and progresses through hope and despair, coupled with relapse and remission, then the eventual loss of the child. Coping with the death of a child is very difficult, at best, even though there may have been the opportunity for anticipatory grief. A great deal of attention has been paid to the effects of anticipatory grief in work with caregivers of Alzheimer's and AIDS patients. At this time, there appears not to be any definitive, empirically validated answer regarding the impact of anticipatory grief on eventual adjustment.

Unanticipated Death

Unanticipated death is sudden and unexpected, thus catching the parent unprepared and perhaps more vulnerable to severe consequences. Common sense alone would lead one to this conclusion. In a study of grieving spouses, Parkes (1975) coined the term "unexpected loss syndrome." The label seems appropriate if one thinks of a syndrome as a cluster of symptoms that occur with some degree of regularity in reaction to a particular phenomenon. Several studies seem to lend support to this contention. Lundin (1984), in a controlled study, found more complicated responses among the sudden death survivors than among those bereaved persons who had not experienced a sudden death. Eight years later, however, there appeared to be no differences between the two groups. Sanders (1989) found that survivors of a sudden death occurrence as well as survivors of a long-term chronic illness suffered severe grief symptoms. This led her to conclude that individuals more likely to adjust to bereavement were those who were grieving the loss of one who had died of a short-term chronic illness. This would suggest that there is an optimum period that allows for some limited amount of anticipatory grief.

The studies cited above were of populations that were not specific to parental grief. The grief experience following the death of a child can be expected to be the same with the exception that the bereavement is more severe in view of the special relationship between parent and child. Several accounts in the grief literature, while not empirical, speak poignantly of the pain of parental bereavement. Many of these accounts are of sudden loss following an accident (Klass, 1988; Sanders, 1986, 1989; Schiff, 1977). In contrast, though, several writers argue that there is no correlation between the outcome of the bereavement and the anticipatory grief experience. It would appear, however, that unanticipated death has a higher probability of engendering severe consequences than death in those situations where there is the opportunity for anticipatory grief.

There are specific types of unanticipated death that are treated in separate chapters in this book. They are violent deaths (e.g., murder or death by a drunk driver) and stigmatized deaths (e.g., suicide or AIDS). In the case of violent death, survivors often feel victimized by both the perpetrator and the legal system (Sprang et al., 1989). In the case of stigmatized death, survivors have their grief disenfranchised. The death is considered shameful and discussion of it is abhorred. When the child's death is stigmatized, parents may believe the death must be concealed, thereby precluding most of the usually sanctioned means of dealing with grief.

The following case vignette illustrates many of the grief reactions that may occur during parental grief. Several of the causal variables are present.

> Mr. G, a 36-year-old senior noncommissioned officer in the military service, came to the attention of the mental hygiene clinic in an overseas country because of inappropriate professional conduct with a subordinate's wife.
>
> Past history is significant. Mr. G had come on this overseas assignment accompanied by his 16-year-old son. Mr. G had been

divorced approximately two years previously, with his wife getting custody of their three children, two younger girls and the boy. Mr. G and his ex-wife agreed to let the son come overseas with Mr. G. The G's had been married 15 years at the time of the divorce.

Two other daughters, aged five and seven, had drowned at the beach while Mr. G was supervising their play in the water. He had been distracted for a short period, and both were pulled into deeper water by a large wave and undercurrent. Both drowned before they could be rescued. Mr. G felt extremely guilty. The G's marriage, which was problematic before, was not able to survive the double tragedy. Their grieving patterns were different, which added to the conflict. Mr. G was a sensitive, feeling person who grieved openly and intensely. Mrs. G, in contrast, was a more stoic, very organized person who busied herself trying to reestablish some equilibrium within the family and seldom openly exhibited grief. Mr. G described an incident a few days after the deaths of the daughters that convinced him his wife did not care. They were accompanying the bodies back to their mutual home on a commercial flight. At an airport enroute, they had to change planes and the coffins of their daughters were removed from the cargo section and allowed to stand on the tarmac in the rain awaiting transfer to the other plane on which they were to continue their flight. Mr. G tearfully related how his daughters were out there in the rain and it seemed that no one cared, not even their mother. Although this had happened three years ago, Mr. G was as pained as if it had happened yesterday.

Prior to the deaths, Mr. G had an outstanding military career, advancing in rank much more rapidly than his peers. From his own assessment, he reported that his job performance for the past couple of years had been barely satisfactory, at best. Some other instances of poor job-related judgment were revealed. His alcohol intake increased markedly. He had repeated dreams about the drownings and the coffins being left in the rain. His marriage failed. He had almost completed work for an undergraduate degree in his off-duty time, but now this had been discontinued. Two things that he continued to enjoy were the relationship with his son and his long-standing interest in classical music.

Arrangements were made for the young worker and his wife to be returned to the United States for duty at a stateside military installation. Mr. G accepted the opportunity for treatment, which included weekly individual psychotherapy and Imipramine 50 milligrams to be taken three times daily. Psychotherapeutic focus was upon his confronting and completing the grief work. It was discovered the son was well aware of Mr. G's struggles and depression, and this partly influenced his decision to accompany his father overseas. Occasionally, the son was seen individually and/or together with the father.

After a period of about two months, there was improvement in the level of depression, while drinking had decreased to an occasional glass of wine or a cocktail. Some four months later, Mr. G went back to school to complete work for his degree. He began to look forward to the completion of his overseas tour of duty and return to the United States, to be followed by retirement shortly thereafter and the start of a second career. He realized his part in the marriage failure, but believed it was beyond reestablishment, and in fact had little desire for reconciliation. A few years later, the therapist and Mr. G accidentally met; at that time Mr. G had remarried, had retired from the military service, and was firmly involved in a satisfying second career. He had fairly frequent contact with his son, ex-wife, and two daughters.

CONCLUSION

There is considerable support for the idea that parental grief is the most difficult that one can experience. Because of its intensity, grieving parents often are seen as grieving pathologically. Efforts are under way, however, to develop a different conceptualization for parents grieving the loss of a child. This seems appropriate. Although there are many similarities in the grief syndrome as it stretches over the wide bereavement spectrum, it differs in a number of ways when the surviving parents are considered. Another case example depicting the special problems associated with parental grief can be found at the end of Chapter 4.

4

The Treatment of Spousal and Parental Grief

The previous chapters have dealt with the most common responses to death: spousal grief, death of the elderly, and parental grief. Other factors impacting the grief response were also considered, such as natural versus unnatural death, suddenness of the death, age of the deceased and of the bereaved, quality of the relationship, and personal characteristics of deceased and bereaved. Approaches to professional intervention may vary depending upon these variables. However, there are some principles that apply when someone seeks help with grief problems or other types of concerns.

Among these are to be empathic, show genuine concern, and to be authentic. Additionally, there is another singularly important aspect, that of the irreversibility of death. Whatever the nature of the relationship at the time of death or the extent of unfinished business, these dimensions cannot be addressed by the two significant persons involved. It may have been a very positive and fulfilling relationship, but the survivor may feel that the satisfying quality of this was never appropriately verbalized to the deceased, thereby leaving an agonizingly empty void. On the other hand, negative and hostile feelings could have existed between the deceased and the survivor and now the opportunity for resolving these issues is no longer available. The survivor may be overwrought with guilt, in part, because our society dictates that one should not harbor negative feelings toward the dead. These types of intervening factors affect the entire grief process.

ESTABLISHING THE PROFESSIONAL RELATIONSHIP

Any hopes for a successful intervention depend first upon establishing a professional relationship that is conducive to effective counseling. Skills that are required in the relationship-building process have been identified under various labels, such as empathy, respect or nonpossessive warmth, and authenticity.

Empathy involves "feeling with" the person, in contrast to sympathy, which implies "feelings for" the person. These two prepositions, *with* and *for*, make a major difference in dealing with the bereaved. "Feeling with" defines a relationship that is understanding, yet objective. "Feeling for," in contrast, creates a high likelihood of subjective enmeshment in the struggles of the client. Death evokes strong emotions; therefore, it is easy for a grief counselor to feel sorry for the bereaved, thus vitiating efforts to move the griever through the bereavement process.

Respecting the dignity and worth of the individual means accepting the right of the person seeking help to follow his or her own course of action in the quest for resolution as long as it is not self-destructive nor infringing upon the rights of others. An example of a self-destructive action would be to allow the bereaved to engage in activities that prolong the grief process.

Authenticity is being honest and genuine with the person who presents with the problem and being with the person physically and psychically. These principles adhere in any help-seeking situation when an individual with a problem requests assistance from a professional helper.

THE CRISIS SITUATION

In the case of the bereaved person, another dimension is added— that is, the death has invariably precipitated a crisis regardless of the circumstances of the death. Whenever a death has occurred recently, one should think crisis and initial efforts should draw upon crisis intervention methods. First and foremost, it is important to realize that a crisis is not a pathological state. Rather, it is something that can happen to anyone at any point in the life cycle. Each person develops ways of coping with everyday living. A "steady state" or level of homeostasis evolves, but when a traumatizing event occurs, the functioning state is disequilibriated. Previously utilized coping mechanisms no longer work.

Considerable variability operates relative to the manner in which different persons handle similar situations, at different points in time. A crisis represents a time when the individual may be particularly responsive to help. In fact, the Chinese symbol for crisis consists of a joining of the characters for both danger and opportunity. The bereaved person can emerge from the pain of the loss as one better equipped to handle future losses or be engulfed in complicated grief or severe depression.

A crisis has five stages: a hazardous event, a vulnerable state, a precipitating factor, a state of active crisis, and a stage of reintegration. Death is the hazardous event; the vulnerable state occurs when the survivor perceived the death as a threat to his or her sense of well-being; if usual coping methods do not handle the tension, anxiety, and stress, the impact of the death is the precipitating factor that triggers the active crisis state; reintegration occurs when the person returns to a level of equilibrium, develops improved coping strategies, or suffers from an inability to adapt (Golan, 1978, pp. 63–71). The crisis paradigm can be diagrammed in the following manner (see Figure 4.1).

It is not expected that the grief work will be completed by the time the bereaved emerges from the active state of crisis, but by viewing the grief response initially within this conceptualization, several gains are achieved. Of critical importance is the fact that the bereavement process is normalized and not labeled as being pathological. The crisis model

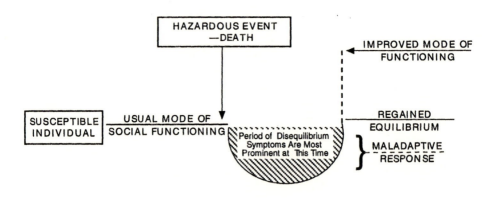

Figure 4.1 Diagram of crisis paradigm

emphasizes the need to allow the distressed person to ventilate to an understanding, empathic listener. Normalization of the grief experience also conveys to the bereaved that such things as the intense pain, agony, intrusive thoughts, physiological symptoms, and feelings of help-lessness are not indicative of losing control or going crazy. This pull of hope, when combined with the push of discomfort, helps mobilize the energy to continue through the stages of grief and to tackle the tasks that must be accomplished to live without the presence of the dead person. Another gain is that early in the intervention process, measur-able milestones of forward movement can be identified.

Although the crisis model addresses some of the particularized needs of grieving clients, the heightened vulnerability should be kept in mind. Every effort should be made to protect them from additional pain and hurt. To some extent, this is begun during the relationship establishment period through the expression of empathy, warmth, and authenticity. There needs to be a climate created that offers solace, encourages and enhances introspection, and allows expression of powerful emotions. The counselor's office may well be one of the few places where there is freedom to cry uncontrollably or to openly vent anger toward the de-ceased. To create this type of atmosphere, Dershimer (1990) recommends the following.

1. Guard against giving dictates and making criticisms, which can add to the client's feelings of shame, guilt, and self-doubt, while further repressing the expression of these and other feelings;
2. Recognize, accept, and validate each emotion as it arises so that clients can move on from one feeling state to another;
3. Be careful not to brush aside, offer platitudes in response to, or judge critically clients' expression of deep-seated fears, doubts, and tumul-tuous feeling;
4. Be patient when clients appear to be stuck in their grief. (pp. 102–103)

Being able to talk about the dead person is important. Friends, family, and others experience discomfort talking about the deceased. There is a tendency not to mention the death, due both to their own discomfort and/or fear of saddening the bereaved. This conspiracy of silence may effectively shut off the pressing desire to talk to someone about the numerous emotions stirred by the loss. Facilitating talk about the de-ceased does not mean the counselor should encourage wallowing in the grief, but appropriate discussion and ventilation are needed. Attention to the needs of the bereaved person is a beginning step in the assessment process.

ASSESSMENT

Assessment (diagnosis) is of value only to the extent that it guides intervention (treatment). An adequate, reliable assessment presupposes the establishment of a trusting, empathic professional relationship with the client. To be useful, the assessment should be multifaceted in nature, including affective, cognitive, behavioral, and physiological dimensions. These, in turn, should include individual focus as well as familial and societal emphases. Many traditional counselors are prone to depend heavily upon intrapsychic phenomena, but this approach seems somewhat limiting in that it minimizes the value of understanding the impact of systems such as the family and larger society upon the grieving individual. Gathering sufficient information to make an adequate assessment requires the use of many modalities; for most counselors this means the clinical interview.

Within the past two decades, a number of Rapid Assessment Instruments (RAIs) have become available to counselors that do not require special training to administer or to score and interpret. Increased recognition of the large role that physiological factors play in the grief process indicates the need, at times, for additional consultation and evaluation by a physician.

The clinical interview is the most commonly used tool of assessment relied upon by the nonmedical practitioner. The interview allows the bereaved to "tell the story" in his or her own way and at a pace that is congruent with needs at the time. A patient counselor can gently guide the interview in a manner that is most productive for both the client and practitioner.

The manner in which the assessment is handled varies also relative to time. If the death occurred recently, then a crisis approach is appropriate. Included within this would be securing information about the circumstances of the death, its suddenness or if there was opportunity for anticipatory grief, any prior significant loss and how it was dealt with, the nature of the relationship with the deceased, and the meaning of the loss for the client. Additionally, the current mental state must be evaluated with particular attention to the likelihood of self-destructive behavior.

Assessment is an ongoing process. After the crisis needs are handled, other important data can be gathered to fill the gaps recognized in the history. Levels of cognitive, affective, and social functioning should be regularly monitored based upon the baseline established during the intake period. Should some concern arise relative to physical symptomatology, referral to a physician is recommended. The clinical interview can, indeed, be used by the skilled practitioner as a vital part of the assessment process.

There are a number of RAIs that can be employed by the practitioner who has not had special training in the use of psychometric tests. One of these is the Geriatric Depression Scale (GDS), which is a 15-item instrument that can be answered in a Yes/No format and administered in five to seven minutes. A clinical cutoff score of 10 or above suggests the presence of depression. Distinguishing complicated mourning from depression is a continuing problem and this scale serves as an aid in this regard.

Another instrument that can be used to measure depression is the Beck Depression Inventory (BDI). This is a 21-item scale that assesses the presence and severity of affective, cognitive, motivational, vegetative, and psychomotor dimensions of depression. The BDI is probably the most widely used scale to assess depression. Higher scores reflect more severe depression.

Several RAIs are available to evaluate cognitive capacity. Among these are the Mental Status Questionnaire (MSQ), Mini-Mental State (MMS), and the Cognitive Capacity Screening Examination (CCSE). Each of these is a pencil-and-paper-administered scale that can be completed within 10 or 15 minutes. Scoring is straightforward and easily understood.

The Impact of Event Scale (IES) measures the stress associated with traumatic events. The specific traumatic event is not specified, but it has been successfully used to assess the impact of the death of a loved one. Two categories of response are measured: intrusive experience such as ideas, feelings, or bad dreams and the recognized avoidance of certain ideas, feelings, and situations. Range of scores on the intrusive experience subscale is 7 to 28 and is 8 to 32 on the avoidance subscale, which indicates the frequency with which either experience occurs. Higher scores indicate more severe impact.

Recently published (1993) was the Grief and Mourning Status Interview and Inventory (GAMSII). This instrument has three major parts: demographic information; comprehensive evaluation of history, mental status, and selected premorbid personality characteristics; and a structured interview that incorporates 10 areas that appear to be important for the understanding of the situation of the bereaved person. This is probably the most global of the instruments indicated above.

Several strategies are available to the practitioner to aid in the assessment process. Mainstay is the clinical interview, but other tools may be used in conjunction. Assessment should point the way to an appropriate intervention plan that distinguishes whether or not professional help is required.

INTERVENTION

The question of whether or not a professional helper is desirable is a perpetual issue. Many practitioners inaccurately assume that the bereaved, especially elderly persons, are socially isolated, depressed, and incapacitated by the loss and perhaps unable to perform the activities of daily living. Lund (1989) has concluded that "many older bereaved spouses do not want or need intervention services" (p. 226). Osterweis, Solomon, and Green (1984) arrived at a similar conclusion, but indicate that everyone needs some education and information about the grief process as well as support and reassurance. Much of this can be provided through informal resources such as family, friends, self-help groups, or lay people. This does not diminish the need, though, to identify those persons at risk for complicated grief problems and to target services to them. Although most persons get through the grief process without professional help, appropriate intervention may facilitate or even help speed up the process.

Timing of helping efforts appears to be of importance. Silverman (1970) coined the term *recoil* in answering the timing question. In a study of bereaved widows, she observed that they were likely to be numb immediately following the death of their spouse, but after three to six weeks they "recoil" and the real meaning of the loss strikes them. This, then, is the optimum time to provide help in experiencing the loss, beginning the necessary role changes, and developing skills to reorder the widow's life.

Recognizing that most spouses successfully negotiate the grief process without the need for professional intervention, the utilization of informal resources should be maximized. The professional can be especially helpful at the primary prevention level by ensuring the availability and acceptability of informal support services that extend beyond family and friends. Examples of these would be self-help groups or the development of educational, information, and referral services. Professionals need to be skilled in crisis intervention that includes specific training in bereavement counseling. Equally important, and in some instances more important, is acceptance of the fact that lay people serving as volunteers have proven to be a very effective resource. Succinctly put, bereavement work is a multidimensional effort that includes empowering the bereaved person, and, in those instances where needed, utilizing professional resources.

Where professional intervention is needed, several tried and proven techniques can be used successfully. As mentioned earlier, the Crisis Intervention model is used frequently during the initial stage of grief. Several other strategies will be discussed below.

Raphael (1984) uses a cognitive approach, Focal Psychotherapy. It relies upon three types of verbal interaction: discussing the relationship with the deceased from the beginning; reporting on what has been happening since the loss; and questioning whether the client has been through similar bad times. The focus is upon three pathological types of grief: inhibited, delayed, or absent. In absent grief, there is no manifestation of grief or mourning. In delayed grief, the process of bereavement is delayed for brief or extended periods of time. In inhibited grief, there is a partial or overall inhibition of the expression of grief. Focal psychotherapy involves getting the bereaved to think and talk about the loss and its cognitive processes so as to experience the pain of the grief.

Volkan (1975) introduced "Re-grief" Therapy. This is an approach that is designed to help the bereaved to remember as well as reexperience the circumstances surrounding the loss. One of the techniques used is that of linking objects. Mementos, clothing, photographs, or other special memorabilia are used to stimulate memories. A major effort in re-grief therapy is to have the bereaved confront the loss, whether it be through conscious material or through dream or fantasy interpretation.

Guided Mourning, a cognitive behavioral approach that was developed by Mawson, Marks, Ramm, and Stern (1981), conceptualizes intervention or complicated grief as phobic avoidance. Guided mourning consists of exposure to painful memories or situations, encouragement to visit avoided places and to say good-bye to the lost object, and exercises such as daily writing and thinking about the death.

Worden (1982) has proposed a model of Grief Therapy. Utilizing his four tasks of mourning, he assesses which of the tasks of mourning the bereaved has not completed. A treatment plan is then developed to facilitate completion of these tasks.

Several other approaches are used that may involve the bereaved alone, family members, or significant others. Psychopharmacologic therapy is also widely used, but there is considerable controversy regarding this treatment method. Arguments against medications are similar to those posed in other situations. Any method that protects the person from the pain of the experience for a protracted amount of time is perhaps unhealthy and serves to extend the time required for resolution.

TREATMENT FOR PARENTAL GRIEF

Strategies for working with bereaved parents such as establishing relationships, conducting an assessment, and engaging in intervention planning are similar in many ways to those necessary for work with bereaved spouses. Three factors must be kept in mind when intervention strategies are considered for parental grief. They are: (1) the severity of parental grief, (2) the duration of parental grief, and (3) the fact that the usual model of grief is not appropriate when one is assessing bereaved parents.

While parental grief is in many ways similar to other types of grief, its severity may reach to such depths that it appears to be pathological in quality. Although no consensus has been reached, for example, regarding the duration of grief following a significant loss, there does seem to be some agreement that parental grief lasts for a longer period of time. When the traditional model of grief that was developed from the spousal grief model is applied, bereaved parents appear to have crossed the border into complicated and/or pathological grief. This poses special problems. Since assessment is of value only to the extent that it guides treatment, an inaccurate assumption of pathology may result in inappropriate intervention strategies. Instead of being helped, the bereaved parent's condition may be worsened or, even more extreme, an iatrogenic illness may be created.

Parental grief is undoubtedly a severe form of grief but does not always necessitate professional intervention. Martinson (1991), in a study of parents whose child had died from cancer, found that almost 75% did not require professional help to deal with their grief. An unanswered dimension, however, is the extent to which the opportunity for anticipatory grief work may have been a confounding variable. Of those remaining parents who sought help, none used more than one type of help. A breakdown of the sources of help is of interest, even though the sample size is small. Over 60% sought help in an organized parents' support group, 17% looked to their minister, 8% consulted a marriage counselor, and the remaining 12% used their physician, a psychologist, or a social worker.

Self-help groups such as The Compassionate Friends or the Candlelighters are by far the most frequently sought sources of assistance. This seems to support the belief that adequate social support systems are reliable predictors of bereavement outcome.

Psychoeducation intervention strategies seem to have the potential to be very helpful when working with the bereaved parents. Psychoeducational methods rely heavily upon the use of groups, but can be utilized with couples, families, or individuals. The important feature is the use of education in addition to support. Bereaved parents need to be educated regarding the dynamics of parental grief. Since the phenomenon is so poorly understood, the bereaved parent is very likely to have been labeled as crazy or losing control. The cognitive and affective components of bereavement are emphasized. This approach empowers the bereaved parents to take control of their mourning. Psychoeducational intervention has been used successfully with families where a member is suffering from a chronic mental illness such as schizophrenia or manic depressive illness. It has also been used with caregivers of Alzheimer's patients. These conditions produce grief and mourning experiences similar to death because caregivers witness the loss of the person they previously knew.

In spite of the fact that parental grief has been called an individual journey, it must be considered from a systems perspective. Each member of the family reacts to the loss in an individual manner, but the entire system is disequilibriated and must be included in the assessment phase and treatment planning. Most important, the family has to reorganize without the physical presence of the deceased person. Often, the parents are so engrossed in their own grieving that they are not available to each other or to the surviving children, producing secondary losses that occur as a consequence of the initial loss. With the deceased missing from the system, the system changes. Roles played by the dead person must be reallocated or absorbed by the system in some fashion. Variations on this may occur if it was the death of a child in a single-parent family. Similarly, there would be differences if the family consisted of a single parent and the deceased child was an only child.

A family systems perspective allows for examination of all the component parts while maintaining the integrity of the whole. Interventions may be planned for the individual members of the family as well for the whole family system. Many of the specific strategies mentioned earlier fit well within this framework. A system approach accommodates long-term as well as short-term interventions and is flexible enough to include individual, dyadic, family, or group approaches.

The present authors encourage strongly the use of a family systems approach. From this perspective, none of the bereaved members are excluded or forgotten. Attention can be focused upon the individual, couple, or nuclear or extended family as the need seems to indicate. In addition, a psychoeducational model is recommended. This format includes a dydactic/educational component, as well as services geared toward the affective needs of the bereaved.

Several self-help organizations are also available that seem to be very

helpful to the bereaved parent. These organizations are so effective because similarly affected individuals are helping one another. Being in
the same boat demands attention in a much different way from that
offered by a professional helper. Among these organizations are:

1. The Compassionate Friends—A self-help group for parents who have
   experienced the death of a child
2. SHARE (Source of Help in Airing and Resolving Experiences)—An
   organization for the comfort and mutual reassurance of parents who
   have lost a baby.
3. NSIDSF (The National Sudden Infant Death Syndrome Foundation)—Its purpose is to provide service to families who have lost
   infants to SIDS.
4. The Candlelighters Childhood Cancer Foundation—A self-help support group for parents whose child has or has had cancer.
5. MADD (Mothers Against Drunk Driving)—This organization has a
   dual purpose: to support victims, their families, and their friends
   following death of a significant other by a drunk driver and to raise
   public awareness about the needless killings that occur due to the
   operation of vehicles by drunk drivers.
6. The Samaritans/Safe Place—The goal of the Samaritans is to prevent
   suicide, while that of the Safe Place is to help survivors through the
   emotional turmoil when a significant other has committed suicide.

Many innovative models have been developed to help the bereaved.
These range from psychodynamic approaches to cognitive-behavioral
methods. Additionally, informal support systems are beneficial, as are
various self-help groups. Whichever method is selected, there is need
for empathic support, education, and availability to the bereaved both
psychically and physically.

The following example, which necessitated professional long-term intervention, demonstrates the use of various strategies in the treatment
of a case of parental grief.

> Gloria, 43 years old, had two children—11 and eight years old.
> The 11-year-old died of meningitis while sleeping next to her in bed.
> Gloria originally presented for counseling three months following
> her daughter's death after being referred by her supervisor for poor
> job performance (increased tardiness, 26 missed days of work, diffi-
> culty concentrating, irritability, and tearfulness at work). Gloria suf-
> fered from extreme guilt: "I shouldn't have fallen asleep. I could have
> saved her. How could I have slept through something like that?"

Her pretest Beck Depression Inventory (BDI) score was 48, indicating a significant level of depression. Her BDI scores continued to stay high (43, 47, 40, 44) over the course of a year. After that time, there was a change in this pattern (22 at 16 months, 17 at 18 months, 30 at the second anniversary of the death). (This illustrates how symptoms vary depending upon the temporal factors and the individual's emotional capacities to deal with the intensities of the feelings.) Gloria had some suicidal ideation and stated, "I want to see her again, even if I have to die to do it."

Gloria had a great need to talk about her daughter and relive some of the details of her death over and over. This made Greg, her husband of 13 years, very uncomfortable, and Gloria felt he was withdrawing from her. She felt isolated and alone. Her husband felt it was best not to dwell on the past but rather to try and put the tragedy behind them for the sake of their other child. Gloria felt anger at Greg for "forgetting about their deceased child," and Greg felt disappointment and resentment toward Gloria for ignoring their living child. Both needed support and compassion, but seemed unable to provide these things for each other out of a need for personal survival.

Treatment: Gloria and Greg both declined family and marital therapy, opting for individual and group work initially. One year following the death of their daughter, the couple separated and entered marital therapy. The initial goals of therapy centered on communication, identifying and verbalizing needs, asking and granting forgiveness, education regarding loss and mourning and the impact on family systems, refocusing on the family, and reestablishing family goals. The couple's other child was enrolled in a sibling class and was included in some of the family sessions, as appropriate. Gloria's discharge BDI score was 12. Considerable time was spent on preparation for the future—setting realistic expectations, preparing for hard times, redefining "normal."

In contrast, the following example of a case of spousal death did not require professional intervention. Mrs. B emerged from the crisis of the death of her husband with effective coping skills, which were buttressed by a strong and reliable support system she frequently utilized.

Mr. and Mrs. B, a couple in their mid-forties with two teenaged sons, seemed to have had everything going for them. Mr. B was the top administrator in a highly visible, political agency. Mrs. B was employed in a state governmental position. They had relocated two years earlier in a move that clearly advanced Mr. B's career. Their family mirrored the idyllic image of the model middle-class family. One son was away in college and the other was progressing well in high school. The family was actively involved in their church as well as in other community activities.

Without warning, the unexpected happened. Mr. B suffered a severe stroke that left him impaired, the most noticeable effect being aphasia. After a relatively brief stay in a hospital and then in a rehabilitation center Mr. B returned home, but remained in rehabilitation therapy for four months, initially on a daily basis, then three times a week. Mrs. B took an extended leave of absence from her job in order to care for him on a 24-hour basis. Mr. B showed considerable improvement and there was high hope for his eventual return to work. Mrs. B prepared to end her leave of absence and return to work, but before this happened Mr. B had a massive heart attack and died before the emergency medical personnel could get him to the hospital.

Mrs. B had shown a total commitment to her spouse's recovery. Now, she was in shock, experienced confusion, and could not believe that Mr. B had died. Although usually very self-reliant, she felt helpless and overwhelmed. Recognizing Mr. B's devotion to his sons, she somehow mustered the inner strength to manage the immediate tasks that had to be accomplished. The church came to her aid, as well as extended family and local friendship networks. She has returned to work, the older son has returned to college, and the teenager has reinvested in school activities.

Mrs. B acknowledges that nights, weekends, and holidays are difficult times. She can talk about her husband now, some nine months later, without being overcome with grief and is able to enjoy occasional social contacts with friends and family. Any major decisions, such as relocating to the previous home, are being delayed until the younger son graduates from high school. At times, she has experienced unexpected episodes of extreme grief and has also had periods of searing loneliness. She has felt some diffuse anger regarding the entire situation, wondering sometimes if the promotional move that advanced Mr. B's career was worth the price, because she believes his death was in large part related to the stress of his job.

Mrs. B has medication for sleep that she uses as needed. Other than seeing a physician for the sleeping medication, Mrs. B has not required professional assistance.

II

TRAUMATIC GRIEF

5

A Theoretical Overview of
Traumatic Grief*

The previous section explored the process of bereavement based upon traditional models of grief. This section introduces and expounds upon yet another significant variable, the mode of death. Specifically, we will discuss the nature and course of bereavement in survivors following a traumatic death. Over the past few years, there has been a growing interest in the psychological plight of the trauma victim. Experts are beginning to recognize that a traumatic death produces indirect victims who suffer intense emotional trauma. Even so, there is little information available regarding the impact of a traumatic death on the psychological adjustment of the survivors. As the number of descriptive studies on death and dying increases, a variability is noted in the grief response of those experiencing traumatic object loss. In the following pages, we discuss the death of a family member due to murder, drunk driving, and community disaster.

TRAUMA DEFINED

It is proposed that the nature and course of bereavement are complicated by its traumatic mode. The unexpected and often violent manner of death in a murder, drunk driving collision, or community disaster adds to both the depth and extent of the psychological response to trauma experienced by the surviving family members. A few authors

*Portions of this chapter were printed with permission from the *Diagnostic and Statistical Manual of Mental Disorders, Fourth Edition.* Copyright 1994 American Psychiatric Association.

(Ochberg, 1988; Parkes & Weiss, 1983) have noted the differential manner in which the mode of death impacts the way individuals grieve. Just how and why these differences occur is a matter not fully explored in the literature, yet clearly it is an issue relevant to accurate understanding and treatment of traumatic grief.

A review of the DSM-IV's depiction of bereavement further underscores the necessity for continued exploration of trauma-related bereavement. It is proposed that there is a lack of conceptual clarity regarding the "normal" course of bereavement when the mode of death is considered.

The DSM-IV describes bereavement as a normal reaction to loss that produces symptomatology consistent with a mood disorder. There is a clear distinction, however, between these depressive symptoms (poor appetite, sleep and appetite disturbance) and more marked impairment in social, occupational, and/or familial functioning. Therefore, pathology is assumed if the reactions to loss are intensified and/or extend beyond these established guidelines for bereavement.

As the following chapters in this section point out, the usual course of bereavement after a traumatic death does not fit the diagnostic criteria for uncomplicated bereavement, nor is the clinical presentation of the mourner easily explained by a sole diagnosis of Major Depression. Can it be assumed, therefore, that most trauma-induced grief is complicated or pathological? As with all perceptions, one's initial reference points are paramount to one's understanding.

Merriam-Webster (1976) defines a trauma as "a painful emotional experience, or shock, often producing a lasting psychic effect and, sometimes, a neurosis" (p. 1513). A traumatic stressor is understood as a stimulus that provokes an overwhelming affective reaction that can jeopardize existing adaptive capacities and impair psychological and physiological functioning. Typically, descriptions of survivor reactions to trauma have been polarized into a dichotomy of symptomatology depicted in grief models (discussed in Chapter 1) or symptoms associated with Post-traumatic Stress Disorder (PTSD). It is believed that a conceptualization of the psychological response to traumatic death is inadequately depicted in either of these models alone.

These ambiguities and diagnostic problems have clinical implications. The process of grief in surviving family members of traumatic death victims may be misunderstood due to the intensity and duration of their reaction to the death. Uncertainty prevails regarding what responses can be expected and what factors influence the extent of the reaction. To address adequately the impact of trauma on the individual and family system, it is necessary to develop clinical intervention strategies, research programs, and social policy based on the proper theoretical framework. Toward this goal, the following presentations explore the components of traumatic grief, then explore symptomatology specific to the mode of death. Implications for assessment and treatment follow. Further clarification and exploration of these variables can lead to the formulation of a new paradigm for understanding this type of trauma.

Generally speaking, the trauma victim experiences reactions consistent with the bereavement paradigm described earlier, yet responses take on an added dimension of PTSD symptomatology. Exploration of the nature of traumatic stress reactions are necessary for adequate understanding of traumatic grief.

In 1941, Kardiner first described the syndrome known today as Posttraumatic Stress Disorder. He noted that individuals with PTSD experienced symptoms consistent with five principal features of the disorder. These categories include: (a) persistence of startle response and irritability; (b) proclivity to aggressive outbursts; (c) fixation on the trauma; (d) constriction of personal functioning; and (e) atypical dreams. These symptoms can be classified into positive and negative clusters, the positive cluster including hyperactivity, aggressive outbursts, exaggerated startle response, and intrusive recollections, while the negative cluster contains symptoms of constriction, social isolation, and a sense of estrangement from family and friends. Forty years later, Kardiner's descriptions were incorporated into the DSM as diagnostic criteria for Posttraumatic Stress Disorder.

> A diagnosis of PTSD is indicated if the person has experienced, witnessed, or was confronted with an event that involved actual or threatened death or serious injury, or a threat to the physical integrity of others, and responded with intense fear, helplessness, or horror. In children, it may be expressed instead by disorganized or agitated behavior (DSM-IV, pp. 427–428).

Criteria B states in DSM-IV that the trauma must be persistently reexperienced in at least one of the following ways:

1. Recurrent and intrusive distress at recollections of the event. In young children, distress may manifest during repetitive play in which themes or aspects of the trauma are expressed.
2. Recurrent distressing dreams or nightmares of the event. In young children, there may be frightening dreams without recognizable content.
3. Sudden acting or feeling as if the traumatic event were recurring, including a sense of reliving the experience via illusions, hallucinations, flashbacks, and dissociative episodes (even those that

occur upon awakening or when intoxicated). In young children, trauma-specific reenactment may occur.

4. Intense psychological distress at exposure to a stimulus that symbolizes or resembles an aspect of the traumatic event (e.g., a specific sound, landmark, date).
5. Physiologic reactivity upon exposure to internal or external cues that symbolize or resemble an aspect of the traumatic event. (p. 428)

The hallmark of Criteria B of the DSM-IV depiction of PTSD symptomatology is the reliving of some aspect of the trauma in some way. Ruminations on the trauma may center around the violent nature of the death or the extent of physical suffering experienced by the deceased. Denial, shock, and psychic numbing can be considered dissociative mechanisms and should be included as symptoms meeting Criteria B of PTSD. These disturbances may be viewed as symptoms of grief and may not be classified as symptoms of PTSD by practitioners inexperienced in trauma work. Therefore, the diagnosis of PTSD may be overlooked. In addition, the existence of Psychogenic Amnesia (see Criteria C) may occur, so that there is an absence of Criteria B.

Criteria C of the DSM-IV description of PTSD describes an avoidance of the stimuli associated with the trauma or numbing of general responsiveness (not present before the trauma), as indicated by at least three of the following:

1. Effort to avoid thoughts or feelings associated with the trauma.
2. Effort to avoid activities or situations that arouse recollection of the trauma.
3. Inability to recall an important aspect of the trauma (psychogenic amnesia). Psychogenic amnesia is produced by dissociation and repression of the traumatic images brought about by affective flooding. The inability to recall may be linked to a specific aspect of the trauma (e.g., death notification). The development of psychogenic amnesia may be linked to a number of variables such as the type of trauma, the fear of future harm experienced by the survivor, and other endogenous and exogenous variables impacting the individual's ability to cope.
4. Markedly diminished interest in significant activities. In young children, there may be a loss of recently acquired developmental skills such as toilet training or language skills. In adults, it is

not uncommon to see social withdrawal and isolation and a loss of interest in previously pleasurable activities.

5. Feelings of detachment or estrangement from others.
6. Restricted ranges of affect.
7. Sense of foreshortened future (e.g., the individual does not expect to have a career, marriage, children, or long life). (p. 428)

Criteria D of the DSM-IV refers to persistent symptoms of increased arousal (not being present before the trauma) as experienced in at least two of the following:

1. Difficulty falling or staying asleep.
2. Irritability or outburst of anger.
3. Difficulty concentrating.
4. Hypervigilance.
5. Exaggerated startle response. (p. 428)

The startle reaction and the hypervigilance symptoms are most common to PTSD and differentiate it from a Generalized Anxiety Disorder diagnosis. Symptoms of hyperarousal and traumatic reexperiencing have been documented in research addressing combat veterans (Kulka et al., 1990), rape victims (Burgess & Holstrom, 1974), kidnapping victims (Terr, 1983), natural disaster victims (Erikson, 1976), and accident victims (Wilkinson, 1983).

Criteria E (p. 429) refers to the time frame of symptomatology and is perhaps the most controversial aspect of the DSM-IV description of the disorder. The DSM-IV suggests that there should be a duration of the disturbance (symptoms B, C, and D) for at least one month, specifying delayed onset if the occurrence of symptoms lasts at least six months after the trauma. Many practitioners interpret this to mean that the individual must have experienced all symptoms (B, C, and D) together within one month for the diagnosis to be made. Others suggest that the duration of each of the symptoms must be one month, but do not believe the symptoms must occur simultaneously.

Some clinicians seem to look at the syndrome as a frozen moment in time instead of viewing the disorder as a flow of symptoms over time, with certain aspects of the event being predominant at different times. Bard and Sangrey (1986) discuss the concept of "waxing and waning of tension," which they found is evident in the crisis reaction of victims of crime. During what Bard and Sangrey call the "recoil phase," the victims they studied experienced intermittent periods of time in which they cognitively, emotionally, behaviorally, and physiologically struggled with the impact of the trauma, and then defended against the feelings by denying them. These two types of activity exemplify the natural process of adaptation to trauma and reintegration of the fragmented sense of self. It is proposed that this unique restorative rhythm is responsible for the variability of symptomatology.

> Criteria F of the DSM-IV requires the disturbance to manifest with significant impairment in social, occupational, or other important areas of functioning. While functional impairment is not uncommon after a traumatic event, these symptoms are generally prolonged after a traumatic death. The disorder is said to be acute if the duration of symptoms is less than three months and chronic if greater than three months (p. 429).

There have also been criticisms of the APA criteria for not being comprehensive in their description of PTSD symptomatology. Other manifestations of the disorder that are not included in the DSM-IV's description of PTSD include:

1. The fear of repetition of the trauma. One indicator of the intensity of the trauma response is the perceived threat of future harm (e.g., a victim who has been threatened with further violence if testifying in court or a survivor-victim who feels unsafe because the perpetrator was not caught).
2. Self-doubt or self-directed anger due to a perceived "failure" to protect loved ones. These reactions may be further influenced by social conditioning, which may dictate certain role performance by specific groups (e.g., males may feel they have failed at their role of protector).
3. Anger and resentment at those exempted from the trauma, at the perpetrator, or at others who were not involved.
4. Survivor guilt about living when those around you have died.
5. A progression of losses after the trauma, such as divorce, loss of a job or home.
6. Morbidity, or an obsession with thoughts of how a loved one felt while dying and concerns about the state and location of the body.
7. Insecurities and self-loathing at one's vulnerability to harm. Feeling a loss of control over one's environment.

Other traumatic grief responses specific to the mode of death will be explored in depth throughout the remainder of this section.

DIMENSIONS OF THE TRAUMATIC GRIEF RESPONSE

The above-mentioned symptomatology illustrates the distinctive nature of the traumatic grief response. The addition of PTSD symptomatology to the typical grief models previously used to understand bereavement provides a more accurate description of the traumatic grief response.

Amick-McMullen, Kilpatrick, Veronen, and Smith (1989) proposed a model that addresses the cognitive, affective, physiological, and behavioral dimensions of the traumatic grief response. Further development of this model provides a general framework for understanding the traumatic grief response.

Cognitive Dimension

The cognitive dimensions of this type of response include ruminations, intrusive thoughts, preoccupation with the loss, confusion, memory impairment, denial, and thoughts of revenge.

Although the research examining cognitive functioning in mourners after a traumatic death is scarce at best, there are a few studies documenting cognitive impairment in other PTSD patients that support the inclusion of this type of symptomatology in the model (Cugley & Savage, 1984; Horowitz, Wiloner, & Alvarez, 1979; Wilkinson, 1983). These findings all report symptoms of memory impairment, memory failure, poor academic performance, difficulty concentrating, and other types of cognitive impairment in their samples. Wilkinson's (1983) study of 102 survivors of the collapse of the Hyatt Regency skywalk noted that 66 of the 102 respondents reporting cognitive impairment were not directly injured by the disaster, but rather were observers or rescuers, supporting the validity of vicarious traumatization.

Although there is some research to suggest the above-mentioned cognitive deficits are not unique to traumatic grief but are comparable to the impairment found in other psychiatric disturbances such as depression and schizophrenia, there is little debate regarding the proclivity in practice to uncover cognitive symptomatology in those suffering from traumatic grief.

Affective Dimension

Affective reactions typically include overwhelming levels of affect as manifested in the presentation of rage, terror, depression, guilt, and irritability. This symptomatology is exhibited beginning with affective acknowledgment of the loss (the emotional release stage of grief) and/ or upon affective reexperiencing of the trauma (Criteria B of PTSD). Affective flooding is a form of reliving some aspect of the traumatic event and is characterized by overwhelming levels of depression, sadness, anger, remorse, or anxiety. Overwhelming effect can be precipitated by cognitive or physiological reexperiencing, symptoms of physiological arousal, or intrusive imagery. Often this flooding is associated with an exaggerated sense of vulnerability and loss of control.

If affective flooding occurs without the intrusive imagery, it is evidence of defensive blocking of the cognitions associated with the overwhelming emotions through repression, denial, psychic numbing, and psychogenic amnesia. This emotional constriction leads to the avoidance symptomatology outlined in Criteria C of the DSM-IV's description of PTSD or denial.

Physiological Dimension

Research is now available (though still preliminary in nature) to support the physiological dimensions of traumatic grief response. The psychobiological aspects of trauma have been considered by numerous theorists and researchers over the last century as the literature concerning PTSD has developed. Freud (1920) clearly addressed this issue when he wrote, "We may tentatively venture to regard the traumatic neurosis as a consequence of an extensive breach being made in the protective shield against stimuli" (p. 91).* Freud goes on to say that traumatic shock causes direct damage to the molecular structure of the Central Nervous System (CNS), which in turn leads to a feeling of helplessness as this stimulus barrier is violated and the CNS is flooded with excitation. Pavlov (1927) suggested that after repeated exposure to trauma, intrinsically nonthreatening cues associated with trauma (the screech of tires or the sound of a car backfiring) become the conditioned stimulus (CS). The CS is then capable of eliciting a defensive reaction, the conditioned response (exaggerated startle response).

Kardiner (1941) used the term *physioneurosis* to describe activities of the Autonomic Nervous System (ANS). In PTSD, the ANS appears to continue to prepare the individual for arousal despite the removal of the stimulus. Measurement of urinary norepinephrine metabolites in Vietnam veterans with PTSD has shown chronic elevation in noradrenergic activity, as compared to control subjects with other psychiatric diag-

---

*The "traumatic neurosis" described by Freud seems to closely resemble the symptomatology presented by those with PTSD diagnoses.

noses (Kulka et al., 1990). It seems the individual may become habituated to the original trauma stimuli, although associated events may cause increased physiological arousal. This increased arousal may lead to increased adrenalin production, which in turn leads to an intensification of all emotional reactions.

With individuals suffering from traumatic grief, feelings of rage and anger are often intensified, and states of hyperarousal can be triggered by somewhat benign stimuli. It may be suggested, therefore, that the intensity of the autonomic arousal in traumatized individuals causes them to go directly from stimulus to response without making the cognitive connection between actual threat and the emergency response. In this way, autonomic arousal no longer acts as a physiological preparation for trauma, but acts as the precipitating agent for fear and an emergency response.

Medical researchers such as Ochberg (1988) have proposed that the avoidance of affective flooding provided by emotional constriction mechanisms is exemplary of an attempt to decrease hyperarousal states via changes in the information-processing functions (decreased levels of information search, conceptual differentiation, flexibility, and persistence). In this way we see the complex interface between the cognitive, affective, and physiological dimension of the trauma response.

Behavioral Dimension

Finally, the behavioral dimension includes phobic avoidance of trauma-related stimuli, increased self-protective behavior, restless hyperreactivity/hyporeactivity, and changes in the utilization of social supports.

Overall, it seems that behavioral manifestations of traumatic grief have a common theme: self-protection of the mourner via cognitive and affectual restrictions and avoidance behaviors. Wilson (1980), in his study of the response of the Vietnam veteran to the death of a fellow soldier, coined the term *purposeful distantiation* to describe the adaptive mechanism developed by the mourner to control the depth and extent of psychic injury by emotional distancing and avoidance of interpersonal relationship development with others. This purposeful distantiation impedes healthy psychosocial growth and development and eventually leads to loneliness and alienation.

Other researchers (Amick-McMullen et al., 1989; Burgess, 1975; Kilpatrick et al., 1987; Sprang et al., 1989) all reference dysfunctional mourning behavior after a traumatic death. As discussed in the following chapters, the behavioral manifestations of a traumatic grief response are of particular importance, as this symptomatology often precipitates the collaboration between client and therapist (e.g., substance abuse, acting-out behavior in children and adolescents), yet can serve as a mask, concealing other psychological and physiological disturbances.

The following case example demonstrates how the cognitive, affective, behavioral, and physiological dimensions of the disorder may be intertwined.

> Margaret is the 54-year-old surviving spouse of Paul (age 55), who was murdered during a convenience store robbery one year prior to her initiation of therapy. Margaret was not present when the shooting occurred, but came upon the body shortly thereafter and notified the police. Margaret complains of short-term memory impairment (i.e., forgetting dates, details, events, birthdays) and is unable to compute simple mathematical equations. She provides evidence of repeated cognitive replay of the events leading to her husband's murder followed by periods of hyperreactivity (probably triggered by a conditioned endorphine release). To combat these periods of hyperarousal, Margaret began self-medicating by consuming up to a fifth of vodka every two to three days. Following these drinking binges she feels helplessness, fear, and rage.

This example illustrates the connection between psychophysiological states and how one disturbance can produce or transform the overall mental health status of the individual.

CONCLUSION

The following chapters in this section of the book will specifically delineate the traumatic grief response based on the mode of death. The reader will note that the manner of dying dictates the nature of the grief response. Each of the following models will follow the traumatic grief typology described above. Though the specific affectual, cognitive, behavioral, and physiological response may vary, there seems to be a similarity in the interface between grief, PTSD symptomatology, and other disorders, regardless of the mode of traumatic death.

6

The Process of Grief
Following a Murder*

As a young clinician armed with comprehensive knowledge of grief
theories and a scholarly understanding of the empirical evidence available on death and dying, the senior author went forth into an initial
therapy session with a 28-year-old client who was seeking assistance in
dealing with the murder of her parents three months prior. The initial
plan was to formulate a treatment program based on a "stage model"
of grief and to provide support and reassurance through a calm and
self-assured presence. This self-confidence was quickly challenged by
the disparity between the textbook depictions of grief and the presenting
symptomatology.

The horror of the events this client had been exposed to over the past
three months and the duration and intensity of her psychophysiological
response to the murder were overwhelming. The realization that the
traumatic nature of the deaths had had a profound impact on the physical, psychological, and spiritual being of the individual created a personal and professional challenge. Personal interest in and study of
traumatic grief began that day and continue to evolve.

This chapter is presented as a description of the process of grief following the murder of a family member or significant other. The evidence
presented is empirical and anecdotal in nature.

Chapter 1 began with a description of the stage theories of grief, the
tasks of mourning, and various debates over definitions and conceptualizations of grief and mourning. Many of these debates have operational
implications, while others seem to be a debate over semantics. This

*The authors would like to thank Roosevelt Wright, Jr., Ph.D. for his contribution to the
empirical work in this chapter.

section of the book describes a distinct typology of grief—traumatic grief. The implications to be drawn from the following discussions should be clinical in nature and should be viewed as a paradigm for understanding reactions to traumatic death. Variations within the model vary according to endogenous and exogenous variables alike.

Descriptions of human psychological processes are complicated by the dynamic nature of the individual, posing significant challenges to clinicians and researchers. The diligence of researchers such as Ochberg, Rynearson, Amick-McMullen, Kilpatrick, Parkes, Weiss, and others brings us closer to identifying and understanding the challenges that face the client and the therapist. An exploration of the cognitive, affective, physiological, and behavioral dimensions of grief following a murder, along with empirical evidence supporting important causal variables in the traumatic grief response, are presented in this chapter.

THE IMPACT OF MURDER

"Thou shalt not kill" is one of the most widely accepted commandments governing human behavior. Murder is the ultimate violation that one individual can impose upon another. The cruelty of this act adds to the depth and extent of the grief experienced by the survivors. Bard and Sangrey (1986) explain that "the survivor-victims are confronted with their own mortality, with proof-positive that they may at any moment, and quite without warning, be deprived of their lives" (p. 22).

This realization is the essence of the psychological disturbance. The myth of personal invulnerability is cultivated and perpetuated by society via seemingly benign methods. The "Santa Claus Myth," for example, promotes the belief in children that good deeds are rewarded by gifts, and misconduct is punished by the withholding of rewards. Adults accept the fantasy of the Santa Claus myth in a good-natured manner, yet hold on to the underlying premise that one's fate and fortune are dictated by one's deeds. Individuals may believe that their status as law-abiding citizens will shield them from random violence. As this belief is shattered, there are some significant losses that occur. The survivor-victim may lose the perception that the world is a meaningful place and may feel estranged and off-balance with the world, losing all sense of right and order.

Secondly, the perception of the self as positive is shattered. Society is often threatened by the sense of vulnerability imposed by crime, and individuals may go to considerable lengths to distance themselves from those "tainted" by this type of tragedy. The mother of a murdered child once stated, "The problem is, Americans are pleasure-oriented and they don't like to be around people who are sad." After the death of her son, she stated that she felt her friends believed she was being punished for her sins. Many of her friends avoided her as if her peril were contagious. She overheard one person impatiently state, "Oh, it was the will of God; she's just going to have to accept it."

In this example, we see evidence of society's attempts to make sense of the senseless by viewing the murder of a child as a punishment for the sins of the mother. Attempts to assign right and order to life's events are inherent in human nature. If attribution can be assigned, then control is restored. For example, if this mother had been a better person, this would not have happened to her. The speaker then decides to make better choices, thus protecting herself and her family from harm. The mourner may be unsuccessful at assigning attribution, thus increasing her sense of vulnerability. Failure to successfully resolve this dilemma can complicate the process of bereavement and impede adaptation.

Ochberg (1988) addresses this phenomenon when he compares the bereavement and victimization processes. "The bereaved feels loss. The victim feels like a loser. The bereaved may feel as if a part of himself or herself has been ripped away. The victim often feels diminished, pushed down in a hierarchy of dominance, exploited and invaded" (p. 11). Further complicating the process of grief resolution is the trauma induced by the interface between the survivor-victim and the criminal justice system.

THE CRIMINAL JUSTICE PROCESS

It has been said that the family and friends of murder victims (and often society as a whole) are victimized twice, first by the criminal and secondly by the criminal justice system. Murder trials often occur two years or longer after the trial. For many survivor-victims, the resolution of their grief and anger cannot be completed until they face that hurdle. Delays and disappointments in the criminal justice process can have a profound effect on grief resolution.

Walster, Walster, and Berscheid (1978) describe the equity theory to explain an individual's reaction to this process. The survivor-victims are confronted with an inequity in their relationship with the perpetrator and the criminal justice system. It is proposed that the extent to which a positive self-image is held by survivor-victims is based on their level of emotional distress and the extent to which they believe they have been treated in an equitable fashion. At the point of victimization, they may feel they have lost all control over their lives. The perception that control and justice will be imposed by the criminal justice system is often shattered by the realities of prison overcrowding, full court dockets, and insensitive court personnel. There is no "goodness of fit" between individuals and the system in which they are forced to interact.

This inequity causes significant psychological distress and a loss of self-image. Amick-McMullen et al. (1989) found that dissatisfaction with the criminal justice system accounted for two-thirds of the variance in anxiety and depression in their sample of 19 family members of murder victims. Additionally, 58% of their sample reported some degree of dissatisfaction with the way the criminal justice system handled their case, while 42% were satisfied. The following quotations from family members of murder victims support these findings:

> "Everyone had a say-so in the prosecution of the murderer by the victim's family. No one asked us what we thought or how we felt. We didn't even know about the trial until the day before. We had no time to prepare ourselves."

> "The perpetrator was allowed to plea bargain for a reduced sentence. He will spend less than two years in prison with good time. My sister got a life sentence."

> "The police never let us know what was going on. We were so afraid, we kept thinking our other children might be in danger as well. Later, we learned an arrest had been made and the man was released on bond. Someone should have told us."

The structure of the criminal justice process does not provide "party status" to family members of murder victims. Therefore the survivor-victims are dependent upon the state to represent their interest via the prosecuting attorney. In reality, the prosecuting attorney is assigned hundreds of cases and may have very little information about the family and/or the deceased, as 90% to 95% of the cases are handled through a plea bargaining agreement. As one Assistant District Attorney states, "I have over 100 cases at a time and it's very disheartening not to get the chance to know the families. I know it seems like I don't care. I do care. I'm just trying to do my job."

In all but a very few cases, survivor-victims will never have their day in court. Many states allow for a Victim Impact Statement to be filed as a means of communicating to the judge, prosecutor, and Board of Pardons and Paroles the impact of the loss upon the social, economic, occupational, and emotional well-being of survivors. To date, this is the only formal point of entry for the survivor-victims into the criminal justice process.

If a trial does occur, survivor-victims may be forced to deal with another series of traumas they may not anticipate or be prepared for. Specifically:

1. If they choose to remain in the courtroom, they will be forced to relive the tragedy in detail over and over from the perspective of all involved.
2. The family and friends may be subjected to graphic crime plots, including horrifying pictures of the deceased.
3. Defense attorneys may attack the character of the deceased in an attempt to deflect the blame from the accused. This process of "blaming the victim" (in an attempt to make the judge or jury feel the deceased was less worthy or "asked for" the attack) can cause significant distress in the survivors, who then feel a need to defend their loved one's honor. Little or no opportunity is provided for this type of rebuttal.
4. Many survivor-victims will come in face-to-face contact with the perpetrator for the first time at the trial. At this time, all of the emotions regarding this individual resurface or may be exacerbated. Many counties provide for a Victim Assistance Coordinator who can be instrumental in preparing survivor-victims for these situations and can even attend the trial with them for support.

Survivor-victims are often overwhelmed by a sense of rage at the perpetrator of the crime. If they do not perceive "justice to be served" by the criminal justice system, they are faced with no lawful means of imposing punishment on the perpetrator. If the criminal is not apprehended, the survivors are deprived of a target for their anger. Absence of a perpetrator or failure of the criminal justice system sets up an "emotional vacuum," often impeding the resolution of anger. A common adaptive mechanism for releasing anger and rage is fantasies of revenge. Poussaint (1984) documents the tendency of survivor-victims to not only ruminate about avenging the death of the loved one but also to try to capture or locate the killer without law enforcement assistance. Although quite alarming to those around the survivor (including the clinician), this can be a useful outlet for dealing with frustration and anger. While common, fantasies of revenge should dissipate along with the anger and rage as the individual progresses through the grief process.

Due to the abruptness of the crime, families forfeit their right to clear up unfinished business with the deceased or to simply say good-bye. The violent nature of the death may further impede trauma resolution by preventing the survivors from viewing the body due to the physical destruction imposed by the crime. Research supports the importance of viewing the body for grief resolution. Outcome studies report prolonged periods of denial and lower total recall of the deceased (after a death from natural causes) in mourners who are unable to view the body prior to burial.

Rinear (1984) outlines the most commonly reported reactions to the violent loss of a loved one. These reactions include: (a) feelings of shock or numbness; (b) preoccupation with loss of the loved one (subjective feeling that part of oneself was gone); (c) concern with the degree of brutality or suffering associated with the crime; (d) anger toward the suspects or criminal justice system; (e) the need to know the details of the death; (f) an appetite disturbance; (g) disturbance of sleep patterns; (h) feelings of depression and hopelessness so intense there is a feeling of unreality; and (i) inability to put the death out of one's mind.

In addition, Rinear found that 34.4% of the respondents in this study reported a negative change in relationships with their spouse, and 27.4% reported a negative change in relationships with their own children. Interpersonal conflicts are not uncommon due to the differential manner in which individuals grieve. No one is provided with a rule book on how to grieve and how to be supportive in a situation such as this. Individuals must find their own way. While there are common characteristics of bereavement, each individual must draw upon a complex set of experiences, and personal and environmental factors, to adapt to adversity. While the factors influencing a response are diverse and unique, some common reactions are noted.

MULTIDIMENSIONAL SYMPTOM FORMULATION

Affective Responses

As described in the Chapter 1, emotional release is exhibited beginning with affective acknowledgment of the loss. After a murder, survivor-victims may experience a prolonged period of shock and denial, which may delay the affectual response. The brutality and abruptness of the death, the police and criminal justice proceedings that ensue, and the stigma attached to the crime set up a propensity for the individual to experience overwhelming levels of affect.

To prevent affectual flooding, the individual exercises repression, denial, psychic numbing, and other forms of emotional constriction to defend against the cognitive process that leads to emotion release. The duration of this phenomenon is unknown, though observation of clients experiencing traumatic grief reveals that this stage of shock and denial may last three to six months initially and may recur at the anniversary of the death or during other significant times such as birthdays or holidays. The affective responses most commonly experienced by survivor-victims after a murder include rage, terror, numbness, feelings of devastation, and irritability.

The distinction between grief and traumatic grief becomes evident. The period of denial is generally prolonged and is followed by an intense, overwhelming affectual response that can last from several months to several years. It is during this period of emotional struggle that interactions with the criminal justice system are most common and most difficult for the survivor-victims, who may "hang on" to their rage at the perpetrator as a means of avoiding some of the intrapersonal philosophical conflicts that arise during the criminal justice process. Common sources of conflict are:

1. Valuing human life, but coming to terms with the "death penalty" as a punishment for the crime.
2. Disparities between biblical interpretations and the criminal justice system's interpretations of justice.
3. Feeling external pressure to forgive a perpetrator who has not asked for forgiveness.
4. How to feel "safe and secure" in an unsafe world.
5. Denying a personal need to resolve emotion out of a sense of loyalty to the deceased.

These intrapersonal conflicts (and others) may impede the resolution of overwhelming emotions, thus increasing the duration of the affectual response.

Cognitive Responses

The cognitive dimensions of this type of response center around the individual's attempts to control overwhelming levels of affect and to make sense out of the tragedy. As described earlier, denial serves as a defense mechanism preventing affectual flooding. These symptoms should also be considered as adaptive to the degree the symptomatology enables the individual to tolerate the intensity of the grief process. Confusion, memory impairment, and an inability to concentrate are induced by the depressive symptomatology associated with traumatic grief. Preoccupation with the loss and thoughts of revenge are attempts to "achieve equilibrium" by making sense of the tragedy and achieving some sense of justice.

These symptoms are an understandable reaction to an event that is generally considered outside the range of normal human experience. Although this symptomatology may contribute to a diagnosis of PTSD, (specifically, avoidance criteria), these responses should be considered maladaptive only if the duration of the response is prolonged and progression through the grief process ceases. Further discussion on adaptive versus maladaptive responses is presented in the treatment chapter of this section (Chapter 9).

Behavioral Responses

After a murder, survivor-victims are confronted with their own mortality. Their increased awareness of their own vulnerability produces a certain degree of anxiety about the safety of one's self and family. Changing routines, purchasing weapons, refusing to go out after dark, and other attempts to prevent further violence are common behavioral reactions. If the perpetrator of the crime is not apprehended, there may be legitimate concerns about the possibility of further harm. The individual's perception of the threat of future harm is an important variable to consider in treatment. Adaptation is impaired as long as this threat exists.

Phobic-avoidance of the trauma-related stimuli is another phenomenon common to traumatic grief. Survivor-victims may engage in "magical thinking," avoiding the scene of the crime (or similar places) as a way of protecting themselves from harm. For example, a father whose daughter was killed after a high school football game refuses to attend and forbids other members of the family from attending any sporting event.

Phobic-avoidance of stimuli can also stem from the anxiety induced by trauma-related stimuli. Survivor-victims may experience physiological symptoms of arousal and anxiety when confronted with traumatic or benign stimuli (e.g., gunshot, car backfiring, or loud noise). Phobic-avoidance of perceived threatening stimuli can lead to social isolation as survivor-victims become increasingly uncomfortable with their environment. This isolation is exacerbated by the tendency of friends and family to distance themselves from the tragic event and/or blame the victim(s). As positive sources of social support begin to diminish, the survivor-victim may begin to withdraw from activities and interactions that were once meaningful. Lack of social support and/or the failure of the survivor-victim to utilize the support that is available is considered to be a significant predictor of traumatic grief disturbance (Koehler, 1990; Ochberg, 1988; Rando, 1984).

Physiological Responses

The physiological dimension of this type of grief can be tied directly to the cognitive, affective, and behavioral manifestations of traumatic grief. The reasons for this phenomenon were explored in detail in the introduction to this section. The most common physiological reactions after the murder of a significant other stem from hyper- and hypoarousal states. These symptoms include appetite and sleep disturbance (Amick-McMullen et al., 1989; Sprang et al. 1989), gastrointestinal, cardiovascular, and immune system changes (Ochberg, 1988), and increased startle response (Kulka et al., 1988; Ochberg, 1988).

Table 6.1 summarizes the affective, cognitive, behavioral, and physiological symptomatology present in the grief response following a murder of a significant other.

CAUSAL VARIABLES

The overall response described above represents a generalized understanding of post-homicide reactions. Of particular clinical significance are those characteristics specific to the individual that dictate the nature, duration, and intensity of the response. An exploration of causal variables is necessary in the development of a comprehensive understanding of the post-homicide grief response.

Although the literature provides a great deal of useful information about death and bereavement, relatively little empirical research has been conducted that attempts to identify those variables that predict the extent of grief experienced by surviving family members of murder (homicide) victims.

As described in Chapter 1, the concepts of mourning and grief have not been clearly explicated. The literature seems to suggest that grief and mourning are discrete, but not necessarily mutually exclusive entities. Grief appears to be dependent upon mourning to begin its process,

TABLE 6.1
Traumatic Grief Symptomatology Following the Murder
of a Significant Other

Affective Responses	*Cognitive Responses*	*Behavioral Responses*	*Physiological Responses*
Anger/rage	Rumination	Social isolation	Sleep
Terror	Thoughts of	and	disturbance
Depression	revenge	avoidance	Appetite
Irritability	Memory loss/	Self-protective	disturbance
Affective flooding	impairment	behavior	Physiological
Numbness	Confusion	Phobic	reexperiencing
Frustration at the	Disorientation	avoidance	of the trauma
criminal justice	Denial	Efforts to	Somatization
system and		pursue and	Physiological
society		capture the	changes in
Emotional		accused	functioning
constriction		Substance	
Feelings of		abuse	
hopelessness		Interpersonal	
and		conflicts	
helplessness			

while mourning is dependent upon the eventual successful resolution of grief. Grief can be conceptualized as the intense emotional suffering that the survivor experiences; as such, it focuses upon internal or affective components. Mourning, in contrast, focuses upon the behavioral or task-oriented activities that are influenced greatly by culture.

The few bereavement studies dealing with traumatic death tend to be qualitative in nature, based on small and inadequately chosen samples, and have been primarily concerned with identifying and describing variables that are associated with normative and/or pathological grief rather than with assessing the relative importance and causal structure of these variables and/or examining the role of mourning in grief resolution. As a result, much of what is known about the grief process is based upon subjective and anecdotal accounts. These accounts provide some useful insights into the existential experiences involved in the process of grief, but they do not lend themselves to the development of the kinds of theoretical models that could provide a better understanding of this complex phenomenon.

To address these weaknesses, a structural equation model has been proposed to delineate the interrelationships among different variables associated with the extent of grief experienced by primary family members after the sudden and unexpected murder of a loved one. The proposed model may be used to identify and evaluate: (a) causes (predictors) of differential levels of grief; (b) the relative importance of those variables included in the model; (c) the magnitude of the direct and indirect causal effects of these variables on grief; and (d) the amount of variation in grief that can be explained within the terms of the model.

Model Specification

The proposed causal relationships among the extent of grief (criterion or dependent variable) and the extent of mourning, the use of social supports, the number of months since the murder, past experience(s) with death, marital status, religiosity, race/ethnicity, age, sex, and annual income (independent variables) are illustrated in Figure 6.1.

Here the variables form a causal chain that follows the order specified in the model itself. That is, the variables of annual income, age, sex, race/ethnicity, marital status, and religiosity (sociodemographic characteristics) are posited to exert *direct* effects upon the use of social supports, the number of months since the murder, past experience(s) with death, the extent of mourning, and the extent of grief. Additionally, sociodemographic variables are posited to exert *indirect* effects upon the level of grief vis-à-vis their direct effects upon the use of social supports, past experience(s) with death, months since the murder, and the extent of mourning. Within the proposed model, sociodemographic variables are treated as exogenous variables because their values are determined by factors that are outside of the model. As a result, the individual and cumulative effects of these variables are controlled, and no attempt has been made to specify any causal ordering or priorities among them.

The variables of past experience(s) with death, the number of months since murder, the use of social supports, and the extent of mourning are treated as endogenous variables in the model (i.e., their values are determined within the terms of the model itself) and are considered to be intervening variables between the sociodemographic variables and the criterion variable, the extent of grief.

The use of social supports, the number of months since the murder, and past experience(s) with death are posited to have direct effect upon the extent of mourning and the extent of grief (Sprang et al., 1989, Zisook & Devaul, 1984; Zisook, Devaul, & Click, 1982). In addition, these variables are posited as having indirect effects upon the extent of grief via their direct effects upon the extent of mourning. Finally, it is posited that the extent of mourning has a direct effect upon the extent of grief without any presumed indirect or spurious effect. In its stated form, therefore, the proposed model posits that the extent of mourning

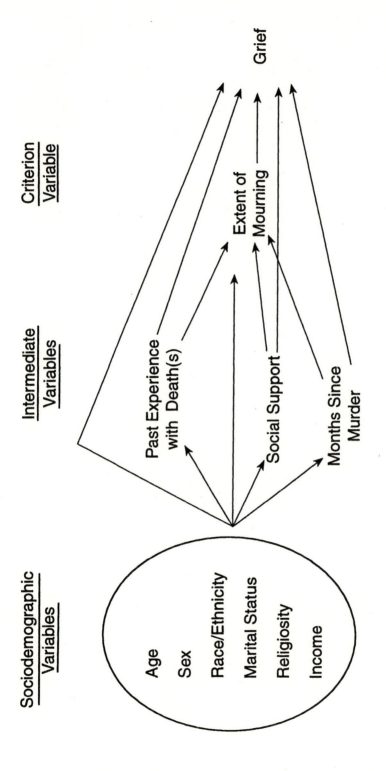

Figure 6.1. The proposed causal model of grief.

is the most important predictor of the extent of grief, and other endogenous and exogenous variables have a secondary role in the grief process.

Each of the variables included in the proposed model has been related previously to the extent of grief in a range of existing studies (Fashingbauer et al., 1977; Kalish & Reynolds, 1976; Koehler, 1990; Sprang et al., 1989; Zisook & Devaul, 1984; Zisook et al., 1982). Moreover, the proposed model forms a recursive causal system that does not include any instantaneous reciprocal or two-way causal relationships among the variables. In this connection, the specified formulation of the model presumes, for example, that extent of grief and extent of mourning are directly affected by the use of social supports, past experience(s) with death, the number of months since the murder, sex, annual income, and so forth, but the reciprocal is not true; that is, age, sex, annual income, past experience(s) with death, the use of social supports, and so forth are not directly affected by the extent of mourning or the extent of grief. The model, as proposed, was transformed into a series of regression equations from which path coefficients (i.e., standardized partial regression coefficients) were estimated.

Methods

The data used to explore the implications of the proposed causal model came from a survey of 101 respondents who were primary family members of murder victims (i.e., spouses, parents, siblings, or children) in the Dallas-Fort Worth, Texas, metropolitan area. The mean age of the sample was 37.2 years.

In terms of the race and ethnicity of the sample, 76.4% were white, 13.9% were black, and 9.7% were of Hispanic origin. With respect to sex, females comprised 51% of the sample, and males comprised 49%. All scales utilized in the study carried high Cronbach's alpha coefficients and are considered reliable and valid indices of the constructs they represented.

Analysis of linear structural (causal) relationships by the method of path analysis was adopted in the present study.

Results

The means and standard deviations for all variables included in the analysis and the zero-order correlation coefficients between the independent variable and the dependent variable (the extent of grief) are presented in Table 6.2. An inspection of the correlation coefficients indicates that six variables (sex, income, marital status, the use of social supports,

TABLE 6.2
Means, Standard Deviations, and Zero-Order Correlations
for all Variables Included in the Model

Variables	M	SD	Zero-Order Correlation
Age	37.2	13.4	.07
Sex	1.5	.5	.26*
Race/ethnicity	1.9	.4	− .05
Income	25(000)	2(000)	.19*
Marital status	2.2	1.2	− .20*
Past experience with death	1.6	.5	− .10
Social support	3.1	1.7	− .25*
Months since murder	27.0	10.0	.16
Mourning	12.5	4.7	.61*
Religiosity	62.1	24.7	.42*
Grief	15.8	7.1	—

*Sig. < .05.

the extent of mourning, and religiosity) are significantly correlated with the extent of grief.

In particular, the data in Table 6.2 suggest that women, nonmarried individuals, those with less income, those who are infrequent or low users of social supports, those who mourn extensively, and those more religiously inclined are statistically more likely to grieve extensively. Additionally, the data indicate that age, race/ethnicity, past experience with death(s), and the number of months since the murder have only negligible and nonsignificant associations with the extent of grief. The absence of significant correlations between these variables and grief is somewhat surprising. Previous research and current thinking on the process of grief hold that these variables function as general correlates of grief (Fashingbauer et al., 1977; Kastenbaum, 1972; Kübler-Ross, 1969; Rando, 1986a).

Table 6.3 presents significant variables identified in the path analysis by gender. More information regarding the examination of correlation coefficients between variables can be obtained from the senior author.

Discussion

In the present study, a multiple-variable structural equation model of the extent of grief among surviving family members of murder victims is proposed. The model is proposed to clarify the correlations among

TABLE 6.3
Significant Variables Identified in the Path Analysis by Gender

	Total Sample	Female Subsample	Male Subsample
Extent of mourning	X	X	X
Use of social supports	X	X	
Religiosity	X	X	
Income	X	X	
Marital status	X		
Sex	X		
Number of months since murder		X	X
Past experience with death			X

'Sig. < .05.

different variables that presumably influence the extent of grief. Like any attempt at model building in the social sciences, it is obviously tentative and, to some extent at least, incomplete in terms of the range of potential variables that could have been included. In the present case, for example, it is apparent that the outcomes of the model would be somewhat different if other explanatory (predictor) variables were introduced, if other modifications were made in the model, or if several alternative formulations of it were considered.

The model presented here assumes, again in common with other attempts at model building, a somewhat rigid structure in terms of the way the variables are related to one another within a framework of one-way causation. Obviously, the causal relationships contained in this particular model could be defined in other ways. For example, the assumption of simultaneous reciprocal effects among some of the variables (i.e., mourning and grief) is perhaps more appropriate than the recursive one-way nature of the proposed formulation. The recursive condition of the proposed specification is, however, characteristic of path analysis as a technique (Kerlinger & Pedhauzer, 1973) and, in this connection: (a) the proposed model should be viewed as a preliminary approximation of a more complex process; (b) the model is limited by the nature of its theoretical assumptions; and (c) the outcomes must be viewed as a heuristic test of these assumptions. Nevertheless, a number of important observations can be made concerning the results.

First, we expected, on the basis of previous research and prevailing beliefs about homicide, to find all of the sociodemographic measures significantly correlated with grief (Rando, 1984, 1986a; Sprang et al.,

1989). Table 6.2 reveals that the correlation coefficients for sex, religiosity, income, and marital status are significantly correlated with the extent of grieving. However, the coefficients for age and race/ethnicity are not significant and, for the most part, indicate a very weak relationship. When the relationships between each sociodemographic variable and the extent of grief are examined using path analysis procedures, the relative unimportance of these variables as predictors becomes obvious (see Figures 6.2, 6.3, and 6.4). Our results, therefore, provide a strong basis for calling into question the efficacy of conceptualizing grief as merely a function of sociodemographic differences.

Second, we expected to find endogenous variables (i.e., months since murder, past experience with death(s), the use of social supports, and the extent of mourning) significantly associated with grief. (See Table 6.2) As Table 6.3 reveals, the use of social supports and the extent of mourning are significantly correlated, but the coefficients for months since murder and past experience with death(s) are not significant. Our results regarding these last two coefficients were surprising in relation to findings reported in previous literature (Fashingbauer et al., 1977; Koehler, 1990; Sprang et al., 1989).

Figure 6.2 presents the final path model for the sample as a whole. Here we see that six variables included in the fully recursive model have significant direct effects on grief. Four of these variables (i.e., sex, income, religiosity, and marital status) represent sociodemographic characteristics and suggest, therefore, that such attributes need to be taken into consideration by grief workers in assisting surviving family members to cope with the death of a murder victim. The remaining two variables (i.e., the use of social supports and the extent of mourning) represent mediating or intervening variables, and of interest here is the observation that they are the best predictors of grief included in the terms of the combined sample model. These findings are partially supportive of previous research (Koehler, 1990; Kübler-Ross, 1969; Sprang et al., 1989) and suggest the need for grief workers to systemically involve the surviving family members in mutual aid or social support networks, which can be effective resources for reducing the extent of mourning and grief and, therefore, should facilitate the loss-adjustment process.

The findings from the present study offer some insightful comparative observations of the different processes at work in accounting for the extent of grief among men and women. For example, the results for the separate analyses for the male and female subsamples (Figures 6.3 and 6.4) indicate that across both subsamples only one variable—the extent of mourning behavior—is a significant direct predictor of the extent of grief. As a causal determinant of grief, the extent of mourning is a

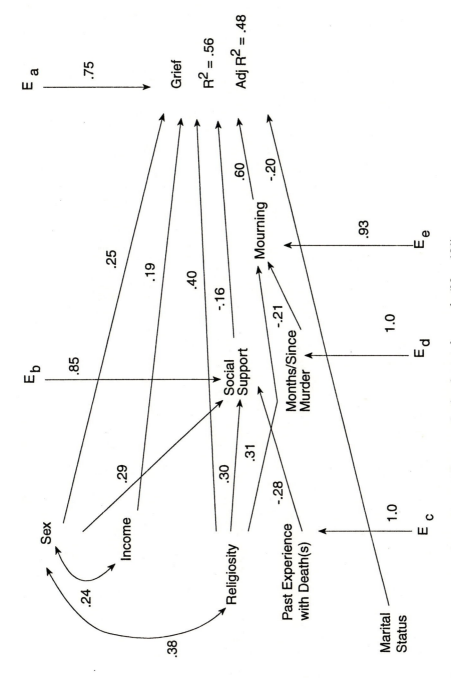

Figure 6.2. Path diagram with significant paths for the total sample ($N = 101$).

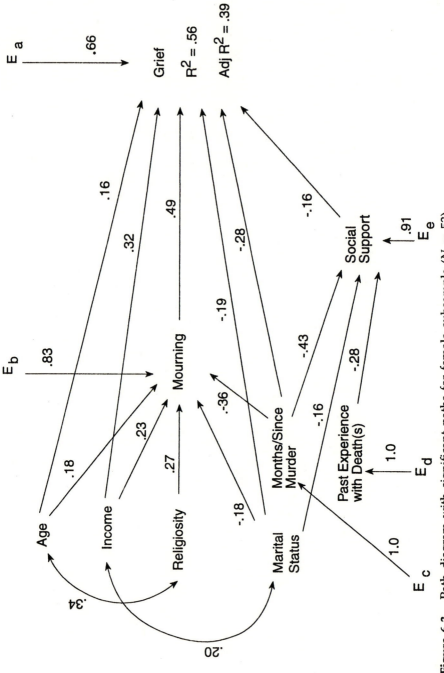

Figure 6.3. Path diagram with significant paths for female subsample (*N* = 53).

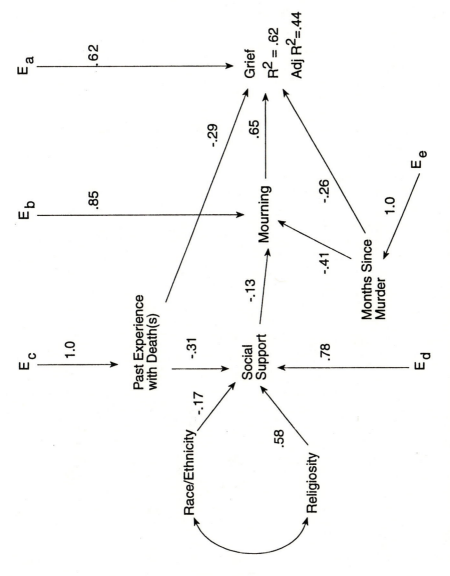

Figure 6.4. Path diagram with significant paths for male subsample ($N = 48$).

more powerful predictor for males than for females, with the path from mourning to grief being .65 for males but only .49 for females.

Additionally, the extent of mourning appears to be a function of the use of social supports and the number of months since the murder for males, whereas, it appears to be a function of religiosity, income, age, and the number of months since the murder for females. Thus, without doubt, the extent of mourning and the extent of grief are far more complex processes for females than for males.

Another major difference between the two groups appears with respect to the role of sociodemographic characteristics. For males, sociodemographic variables appear to be of minor importance, but for females they play a much more pronounced role in explaining grief. Among males, for example, the sociodemographic variables are important only with reference to other mitigating or intervening variables that directly affect grief. For females, however, the sociodemographic variables directly and indirectly influence the level of grief.

Differences between males and females also appear with respect to the role of the social support system. For females, the use of social supports (including support by the spouse) is a relatively potent factor affecting the extent of grief. For males, however, the use of social supports is of secondary importance in reducing the extent of grief (i.e., its effect on grief is translated through the extent of the mourning variable).

Another apparent difference between the groups is the roles that the endogenous or mediating variables play. For males, endogenous variables are the only direct predictors of grief (i.e., past experience with death(s), the number of months since the murder, and the extent of mourning), whereas for females, only three of the six predictors of grief are endogenous (the use of social supports, the extent of mourning, and the number of months since the murder). These findings are extremely important because, for the most part, mediating (endogenous) variables (i.e., personality and psychological factors) have not been adequately addressed in previous research. Additionally, research has not addressed those areas of life that are affected by differences in personality and psychological characteristics between males and females and the manner in which these characteristics have significant consequences on their differential responses to grief.

The emergence of the extent of mourning as the optimum predictor of grief across all models is not surprising and supports the view that symptoms or feelings that are predictive of grief may be viewed as subjective responses to a range of internal and/or external stimuli. The extent of grief, therefore, becomes the end product of the interrelationships between various social and psychological factors as specified in the different models (Figures 6.2, 6.3, and 6.4).

In this conjunction, it seems reasonable to suggest that self-judgments of the extent of grief are primarily derived from psychological factors or internal perceptual states. That is, self-assessments of grief involve processes whereby psychological, personality, and subjective (perceptual) information is brought into play. It is not altogether clear, however, what other types of information are drawn upon by surviving family members. It may be the case that in addition to psychological or perceptual information, some family members (particularly surviving females) tend to also consider other, more objective information pertaining to aspects of their present life situations (age, income, marital status, etc.) when evaluating the extent to which they experienced grief after their losses. To the extent that psychological and internal states are stable features of the survivors, grief may be a relatively immutable phenomenon.

In summary, the findings reported in this study provide a strong basis for exposing the myth that grief is an invariant phenomenon across different subgroups. Our data clearly indicate that there are structural variations in the patterns of grief between males and females.

In this connection, it would be interesting to explore additional variables of the proposed model across other subpopulations (e.g., in terms of age and race/ethnicity). If, in fact, other structural variations are uncovered, this information would be especially useful in the development of empirically based intervention approaches that could be much more effective in facilitating successful completion of the process of traumatic grief. Furthermore, the present study should be replicated. In this manner, the robustness of the parameter estimates can be evaluated and the extent to which the findings are generalizable can be assessed.

7

The Process of Grief Following a Drunk Driving Fatality

In a recent year in the United States, 19,900 people were killed by intoxicated drivers (National Highway Traffic Safety Administration, 1992). More than 48% of all 16- to 20-year-olds killed in a motor vehicle accident (MVA) died as a result of a drunk driver. In the past decade four times as many Americans died in drunk driving crashes as were killed in the Vietnam War. This crime knows no socioeconomic boundaries and shows no respect for age, race, gender, or political persuasion. There is no realistic means of safeguarding oneself or loved ones from the possibility of becoming victimized by a drunk driver.

The deaths produced by drunk driving collisions have been analyzed primarily in terms of a demographic study of events directly related to the collision (who, what, when, where, and how). The conceptual understanding of the grief response relative to this mode of death is a variable that is complex and often misunderstood. This chapter will provide a discussion of a typology of grief inherent to the bereavement process following the death of a loved one in a drunk driving accident. As a means of model development, predictor variables will be examined and significant relationships will be noted.

The reader will take note of two important conceptual distinctions: 1. accident versus crime; 2. crime versus social problem. Traditionally, any collision involving a motor vehicle has been termed a "motor vehicle accident." Police officers rush to the "accident scene," conduct an "accident investigation," write an "accident report," determine the cause of the collision, and attribute blame accordingly. However, in a collision involving a drunk driver, some semantic distinctions should be considered.

Arrests for driving under the influence (DUI) or driving while intoxicated (DWI) accounted for the highest (1.8 million) arrest count in 1990, followed by larceny theft (1.6 million) and drug abuse (1.1 million) (Federal Bureau of Investigation, 1991). Advocacy groups such as Mothers Against Drunk Driving have done a tremendous job, with the help of the media, law enforcement, and public and private school systems, of promoting education and awareness about the impact of alcohol and drugs on an individual's ability to drive. Is it reasonable to assume that a drunk driving fatality is an accident? Some may argue that the lack of intent to do harm provides justification of the crime as an accident or an "involuntary act." Even so, those who fail to control their own behavior (drinking and driving), knowing the behavior to be dangerous, transform an act of omission into an act of committing a crime. Therefore, the term "drunk driving accident" is improper and misleading, serving to minimize or distort the meaning and/or one's understanding of the death and, therefore, of the death response.

Further complicating the issue is the tendency to view the problem of drinking and driving as a social problem rather than a crime. In many states the punishment for property crimes (theft, etc.) are harsher than those for involuntary manslaughter (with intoxication). Many individuals convicted of negligent homicide or involuntary manslaughter are eligible to receive probated sentences and may never serve any jail time at all. About half of the persons jailed for DWI have had previous DWI convictions (Bureau of Justice Statistics, 1988). In 1991, over 318,000 persons suffered injuries in crashes where police reported alcohol was present, an average of one person every one and a half minutes. About 84,000 of these were serious injuries (NHTSA, 1992).

In cases where death does not occur, regardless of the severity of the injuries, many states consider the crime to be a misdemeanor. Victims may remain comatose for life or may never recover from their injuries, leaving a group of survivors who suffer perhaps the most traumatic loss of all. In these cases, the inequity in the interface between the criminal justice system, the perpetrator, and the survivors produces a disequilibrium that can be socially, emotionally, and financially devastating. The process of grief is both impeded and exacerbated by the prolonged struggle with the effects of the trauma.

There is growing public sympathy for those who suffer from chemical addictions. The disease concept of addictions may lead to the premise that the crimes committed while under the influence of a substance are a symptom of the disease over which the individual had no control.

While the disease concept of addictions is not challenged, the lack of assigned culpability complicates the grief process for the mourners by creating a situation in which the mourner is discouraged from healthy expression of anger toward the perpetrator. The following case example illustrates this problem.

> Ray entered therapy 12 months after his wife, Barbara, had been killed by a drunk driver while walking the family dog on a residential street near their home. Ray was complaining of insomnia and gastrointestinal difficulties of unknown etiology. Ray's physician had not been able to find anything physically wrong with him. Ray also reported interpersonal conflict with his coworkers and family resulting from disagreements regarding Ray's involvement in the criminal prosecution of the drunk driver who had killed Barbara. The family reportedly views the perpetrator as a victim of the disease of alcoholism and feels the Christian thing to do is to forgive and forget. After numerous arguments over Ray's efforts to assist in the pursuit and punishment of the criminal, he has withdrawn from all contact with his family or criminal justice personnel. Ray reported he feels guilty for not controlling his emotions better and has tried to put the whole thing out of his mind.

By denying his feelings, Ray is denying himself the opportunity to grieve. Anger is an expected aspect of traumatic grief, so repression of "normal" feelings serves only to prolong the resolution of grief. While the strategy of "forgive and forget" may or may not have served the family's emotional interests well, it has clearly become maladaptive for Ray, as evidenced by the somatization, interpersonal conflicts, and insomnia.

Drunk driving fatalities are unnatural and senseless in nature. Loss of life due to an overindulgence in chemicals is an unnecessary waste of life. Survivor-victims experience outrage at the perceived selfishness of the perpetrator, who they believe valued a "good time" over the safety of others. However, collisions are sudden, unexpected, and violent in nature, thereby increasing the sense of vulnerability experienced by the survivor-victim.

The physical destruction of the body caused by the crash and/or subsequent fire may prevent the mourner's identification of the body. Acceptance of the death may be impeded or prolonged in these cases. Many mourners ruminate about the physical status of the body at the time of death. Some clients even report experiencing physical pain similar to that which they imagine their loved one enduring prior to death. The concept of attribution is of significance because of the social and legal controversy surrounding the perception of culpability in drunk driving collisions. The survivor-victim may feel a need to assign blame as a means of restoring personal equilibrium (see Chapter 10 for a further discussion of personal invulnerability), yet may feel that society and/or the legal system are minimizing the significance of the perpetrator's responsibility. These interpersonal/environmental conflicts lead too often to overwhelming feelings of frustration and anger, which exacerbate the process of grief.

A drunk driving fatality provokes a series of losses for the survivor-victim that extend beyond the loss of life and complicate the adaptive process.

1. Loss of self-esteem—Many survivor-victims (especially parents) may feel they have failed to protect their loved one from harm and may hold themselves responsible for not preventing the death. The result is increasing levels of hopelessness and helplessness that are exacerbated by the criminal justice system and by societal responses.
2. Loss of sense of security—The myth of invulnerability is shattered, and survivor-victims must learn to redefine normal and reformulate personal boundaries.
3. Loss of relationship—This loss applies regardless of whether a death occurred or whether the victim was injured. The trauma produces significant systemic changes that affect the nature and course of relationships in all those impacted by the trauma (i.e., divorces, estrangement, separation).
4. Loss of identity—Individuals are defined, in part, by the roles they assume. Role theory can be utilized to explain this phenomenon. Davis (1986) states, "Social identity is the sense of ourselves that we occupy and the adequacy with which we and significant others judge our role performance" (p. 546). This concept, when applied to roles and relationships after a traumatic death, implies that our sense of self-identity is damaged by a perceived failure to adequately fulfill the role expectations dictated by society. A parent whose child is killed in a drunk driving collision may feel he or she has failed in the role of a parent by not protecting the child or preventing the crash. A spouse who loses a partner is unable to continue in the role of mate, leaving him or her feeling lost and confused. A child who loses a parent may egocentrically assume that some mistake or misdeed he committed caused the parent to go away. The result is the child feels ashamed and rejected. In each of these examples, the survivor-victim personalizes the tragedy and tries to integrate the event into his/her sense of self. The result is disorganization and distress until

the survivor-victim is able to redefine the sense of self in light of the trauma.

Although driving under the influence of a substance is a crime, killing someone with a car seems to be more socially and legally acceptable than murder by other means. The validity of these assumptions may be challenged, but the importance and significance of these issues to the mourners must not be minimized or ignored.

MULTIDIMENSIONAL SYMPTOM FORMULATION

The typology of grief after a drunk driving collision is similar to that of grief after a murder. This typology both impedes and exacerbates the process of grief, depending upon the affective, cognitive, behavioral, and physiological manifestations of the event in the individual survivor. In general, this typology of grief includes the symptomatology shown in Table 7.1.

The reader may note that the manifestation of loss after a drunk driving collision produces symptomatology consistent with Post-traumatic Stress Disorder (PTSD) and grief theories. It is at this point that the con-

TABLE 7.1
Symptomatology of Grief

Affective Responses	*Cognitive Responses*	*Behavioral Responses*	*Physiological Responses*
Anger/rage	Rumination	Social isolation	Sleep and appetite
Terror	Thoughts of	and avoidance	disturbance
Depression	revenge	Self-protective	Physiological
Irritability	Memory	behavior	arousal
Numbness	impairment	Phobic	Physiological
Affective	Confusion	avoidance of	reexperiencing
flooding	Disorientation	painful and	of the trauma
Frustration at the	Denial	benign stimuli	Somatization
criminal justice		Efforts to	Physiological
system and		pursue and	changes in
society		capture the	functioning
Emotional		accused	
constriction		Interpersonal	
Feelings of		conflicts	
hopelessness		Substance abuse	
and			
helplessness			

sideration of traumatic grief should include an examination of the applicability of certain conceptual models included in the study of trauma and grief. A dichotomization of these models fails to adequately depict the response of a survivor-victim. As the literature in this area is still exploratory in nature, the following study was developed to determine if the development of a new conceptual model to describe the post-trauma response is warranted. The following research questions are addressed:

1. Do the symptoms described in the grief models and PTSD symptomatology have some predictors?
2. What proportion of survivor-victims suffer from PTSD in addition to symptoms of grief?
3. What is the impact of variables such as gender, social support, religious beliefs, subjective health status, time since death, and past experience with death on the grief process and formation of PTSD symptomatology?

The answers to these questions provide a framework for understanding traumatic grief after a drunk driving collision. Although the results are not generalizable to grief processes linked to other modes of death, the findings provide significant directives for future study.

Methods

Participants in the study were selected from support groups, social service organizations, and agencies throughout Texas.* Those included were spouses, parents, siblings, or children of a deceased drunk-driving victim. The time since death ranged from one to 60 months, with 28 months being the mean. Of those surveyed, 77.2% had not experienced another death within five years. A survey questionnaire containing demographic data, an extent of mourning scale, an extent of grieving scale, a religious beliefs scale, a social support scale, and a scale measuring levels of PTSD was mailed to the 312 individuals selected for inclusion in the study. There were 171 questionnaires completed and returned for a response rate of 55%.**

---

*The average age for participants in the study was 38.9 years. The majority of the respondents were female (54.4%), while 45.6% were male; 60% were white, 28.7% were black, 7% were hispanic, and 4% were categorized as other.

**The instruments used in this study carry high reliability and validity ratings. Further information regarding sampling or measurement procedures can be obtained from the senior author.

Measurement Procedures

Descriptive statistics were used to provide an overview of the variable distribution in the study sample. Multiple regression techniques were employed to determine the extent to which gender, age, race, subjective health status, income, marital status, past experiences with death, time since death, religious beliefs, and social support—controlling for the effects of other variables in the equation—singularly and in combination accounted for variance in the following criterion variables: (a) the extent of mourning; (b) the extent of grieving; and (c) the level of PTSD symptomatology. Multiple regression procedures provide a standardized partial regression coefficient, which represents the change that would take place in the criterion variable, given a one-unit change in the independent variable. This may be viewed as the direct effect or beta weight of the predictor variable, controlling for the effects of all other variables in the regression equation.

A decomposition technique was used to dissect the zero-order correlation coefficient (see Table 7.2) between each predictor (independent) variable and the main criterion (dependent) variables. The results are then represented in tabular form in Table 7.3 and are conceptualized as total effect values (correlation coefficients), direct effect values (standardized partial regression coefficients or beta weights), and indirect values (correlation coefficients minus beta weights).

T-test procedures were utilized to assess the difference in mean scores between males and females on the criterion variables: (a) the extent of

TABLE 7.2
Zero-Order Correlations Between Select Independent Variables
and the Dependent

Independent Variable	Dependent Variable	R
Subjective health status	Extent of mourning	− .466**
	PTSD	.312**
	Extent of grieving	− .308*
Social support	Extent of mourning	− .504**
	Extent of grieving	− .547**
	PTSD	.783**
Religious beliefs	Extent of grieving	.476**
	Extent of mourning	.590**
	PTSD	− .610**

*Indicates significance at .05 level.
**Indicates significance at .001 level.

TABLE 7.3
**Decomposition Table Illustrating Total Associations, Direct Effects,
and Total Indirect Effects of the Significant Relationships**

Dependent Variable of the Coefficient of Determination (R^2)	Independent Variable	Total Association (r value)	Direct Effect (beta)	Total Indirect Effect
PTSD	Social support	.783	.415**	.368
($R^2 = .82$**)	Gender	.325	.247**	.078
	Subjective health status	.312	.173**	.139
	Religious beliefs	− .610	.155*	− .455
Extent of mourning	Social support	− .504	− .350**	− .154
($R^2 = .57$**)	Subjective health status	− .466	− .344*	− .122
	Religious beliefs	.590	.272**	.318
	Race	− .236	− .156	− .080
	Marital status	− .184	− .131*	− .053
Extent of grieving	Social support	− .547	− .479**	− .068
($R^2 = .44$**)	Religious beliefs	.478	.204**	.272
	Subjective health status	.308	− .206*	− .102

*Indicates significance at .05 level.
**Indicates significance at .001 level.

mourning; (b) the extent of grieving; and (c) the level of PTSD symptomatology.

The .05 level of significance was employed throughout the analyses as a criterion for rejecting the null hypotheses.

This study produced the following results:

- The better the individual's perceived health, the lower the extent of mourning behaviors reported, the lower the level of grieving, and the lower the level of PTSD symptomatology experienced.
- Increased levels of social support utilization lead to increases in the extent of mourning, the extent of grieving, and the levels of PTSD reported.
- Increased religiosity led to decreases in the extent of mourning, the extent of grieving, and the level of PTSD reported. These results do not vary by gender.
- Females reported higher levels of grieving and PTSD than males. There were no differences in the extent of mourning by gender.
- Interestingly, there was no significant relationship between the time

since death, the extent of mourning, the extent of grieving, and PTSD symptomatology.
- A multiple regression analysis of the variable, extent of mourning, indicated that the level of religious beliefs accounted for 34.8% of the variance in the level of mourning, with those reporting lower levels of religiosity experiencing increases in mourning behavior. Social support and health each explained less than 10% of the variance. Table 7.4 illustrates the direct effects and explained variance accounted for in significant variables for the extent of mourning.
- The strongest predictor of the extent of grieving was determined to be social support (29.9% of the variance in the extent of grieving scores). Religious beliefs and subjective health status accounted for less than 10% of the variance in this variable. Table 7.5 demonstrates the direct effects and the explained variance accounted for in significant variables for the extent of grieving.
- Four variables were found to be significant predicators of PTSD symptomatology: social support (43.2% of the variance), subjective health status (13.3% of the variance), religious beliefs (10.6% of the variance), and gender (4.2% of the variance, with females reporting higher levels of PTSD than men). Table 7.6 illustrates the direct effects and explained variance accounted for in all significant variables for the level of PTSD symptomatology.

TABLE 7.4
Direct Effects and Explained Variance Accounted For in Significant Independent Variables for the Extent of Mourning

Dependent Variable	Independent Variable	Direct Effect	Explained Variance Accounted For
Extent of mourning	Religious beliefs	.272**	34.8%
	Social support	− .350**	5.0%
	Subjective health status	− .344**	8.27%
	Race	− .156*	1.8%
	Marital status	− .131*	1.67%
Total variance accounted for			57.5%

*Indicates significance at .05 level.
**Indicates significance at .001 level.

TABLE 7.5
Direct Effects and Explained Variance Accounted For in Significant
Independent Variables for the Extent of Grieving

Dependent Variable	Independent Variable	Direct Effect	Explained Variance Accounted For
Extent of grieving	Social support	− .479*	29.9%
	Religious beliefs	.204	5.37%
	Subjective health status	− .206*	8.27%
Total variance accounted for			44.5%

*Indicates significance at .0001 level.

Discussion

An examination of variables points to the significance of gender, health, level of religious beliefs, and social support in understanding and predicting the extent of mourning, the extent of grieving, and PTSD symptomatology. Multivariate analysis demonstrates that health, social support, and religious beliefs share predictive value for the dependent variables presented in this study, with gender demonstrating predictive power for PTSD symptomatology only.

The level of social support perceived by the respondent proved one of the strongest predictors of all three dependent variables. Respondents who reported high levels of social support had lower levels of mourning, grieving, and PTSD symptomatology. The level of attachment, social

TABLE 7.6
Direct Effects and Explained Variance Accounted For in Significant
Independent Variables for the Level of PTSD Symptomatology

Dependent Variable	Independent Variable	Direct Effect	Explained Variance Accounted For
PTSD	Social support	.415*	43.2%
	Subjective health status	.173*	13.3%
	Gender	.247*	4.2%
	Religious beliefs	− .155*	10.6%
Total variance accounted for			76.9%

*Indicates significance at .001 level.

integration, reassurance of worth, and the presence of reliable alliance and guidance (tapped by the Provisions for Social Relations Scale) are important deterrents to the social isolation that is common after a family member is killed in a DWI collision. This finding supports Turner, Frankel, and Levin's (1983) theory, which postulates that the more isolated an individual is, the more complicated and prolonged the grief.

The significant relationships between religious beliefs and the extent of mourning, the extent of grieving, and PTSD symptomatology indicate that the more religious an individual is, the lower the level of mourning, grieving, and PTSD symptoms reported. These findings suggest that religious beliefs aid in adaptation and resolution of trauma and are in keeping with Rinear's (1984) study, which reported that 20% of the respondents (who had a loved one killed in a violent crime) experienced a positive change in their religious beliefs after the crime.

It is possible that the following beliefs, as measured by a religion scale, provide the individual with the cognitive and behavioral skills necessary for successful adaptation to trauma: (a) the idea of a relationship with a supernatural being; (b) the idea of the relation of human beings to the conception of nature; (c) possession of a set of religious doctrines concerning reciprocal duties and relationships between divinity and humanity; and (d) a set of behavior patterns designed to conform to the will of God and ensure the individual believer the approval of a conscience. The death may be perceived as a "test of faith" or "part of God's divine plan." Others may draw on the relationship with God and the church as a source of social support. Finally, the spiritual doctrines outline acceptable behavior and may be adopted in faith by the individual in absence of other coping strategies. Although some literature suggests there may be an initial crisis of faith (Harris, Sprang, & Komsak, 1987; Lord, 1987), these findings suggest that those whose faith is preserved or who have a restoration of faith have fewer symptoms of distress arising from the death of a family member in a drunk driving collision.

Individuals who rated their health as poorer had higher levels of mourning, grieving, and PTSD symptoms. This finding is in keeping with previous descriptions of the grief process and the DSM-IV description of PTSD, as well as supporting the physiological dimensions of these theories. Physiological reexperiencing and arousal and somatization are often manifestations of this type of trauma and may have contributed to the respondent's perceived poor health at the time of the study.

When gender was used to categorize the respondents, males and females varied in their scores on the extent of mourning, extent of grieving, and PTSD scales. While males reported higher levels of mourning at the time of death, females had higher levels of grief at the time of responding and reported higher levels of PTSD symptomatology. Although multivariate analysis proved no strong predictive value for gender in accounting for variance in extent of mourning, gender explained a significant share of the variance in scores on the PTSD scale, with females scoring significantly higher on the M-PTSD than males.

In light of the findings presented in this study, the reaction to the death of a family member who was killed in a drunk driving collision appears to be the interrelationship between personality, social, psychological, and physical factors that influence the responses to grief. The differential response patterns of males and females in their self-assessments indicate that the above-mentioned factors are drawn upon in the response to trauma. The process of trauma resolution is certainly different for males and females, though the nature of these differences and the stability of these characteristics is unknown, since such endogenous variables have not been adequately addressed by research.

The findings in this study suggest that race and marital status account for 1.8% and 1.67%, respectively, of the explained variance in the extent of mourning. The significance of marital status is likely related to the provision of social support in the marriage. As 63.7% of the respondents were married at the time of the study, there may be an intercorrelation between the variables of social support and marital status. These findings highlight the importance of therapy utilizing a systems approach to address factors influencing the marriage and family system as a means of facilitating social support.

The significance of the variable of race suggests there may be racial and cultural variations in the way individuals mourn. The findings in this study indicate that white respondents reported lower levels of mourning than nonwhites. These differences may be due to cultural/racial factors impacting the individual's psychological adaptation. Further research is needed to determine which racial/cultural variables significantly impact the response to trauma. This type of study will aid in the development of treatment intervention strategies aimed at service delivery that is sensitive to racial/cultural differences.

It is conceivable that historical factors may have introduced a source of bias and jeopardized the internal validity of the study. If the respondents were involved in or anticipating the trial of the accused, or if recent case developments were unfavorable, responses to information solicited by the questionnaire may be distorted by recent events. Additionally, the accuracy of this information may be called into question. The instrument asks respondents to recall feelings and behaviors associated with a very painful time. In this way, maturation effects may have changed the responses. However, responses to the questionnaire items are consistent with information gathered during personal interviews and are believed to be accurate representations of the individual's response to trauma.

Future research is indicated to determine the degree to which the combination of symptomatology complicates and exacerbates grief responses. Examination of simultaneous reciprocal effects among variables such as health, social support, gender, and religion would provide a causal framework for understanding the relationships between the variables. Due to the complexity of grief, the range of potential variables is vast, and the variables included in this study may be incomplete. The inclusion of other variables may mitigate future findings.

CONCLUSION

Post-trauma grief after a drunk-driving-related death produces symptomatology consistent with grief and PTSD models. It would seem that future progress in the treatment of clients suffering with this type of traumatic grief rests in the collaborative efforts of professional researchers, policy makers, therapists, and the testimonies of those experiencing the trauma. The exploration of factors influencing the post-trauma response is the first step in addressing the deleterious social impact of a drunk driving fatality on the grieving process.

8

The Process of Grief Following a Death from a Community Disaster or Critical Incident

This chapter deals with grief responses following death caused by two types of traumatic events—community disasters and critical incidents. Community disasters may be caused by natural events (floods, hurricanes, etc.) or by man-made events such as fires caused by arson. Critical incidents generally refer to work-related disasters such as an explosion at an oil refinery or collapse of a mine that most directly impact a set of employees at their workplace. Similarities and differences in the psychological impact of these events on the mourner are discussed throughout this chapter.

In each of these events, the grief response is influenced by a cataclysmic phenomenon: a sudden and powerful set of events that severely tax the adaptive abilities of those who are exposed. The reactions may be acute or chronic depending on the nature of the precipitating event and the environment of the individual. The acuity or chronicity of the response is of prognostic value in determining the course and duration of the traumatic grief reaction. The purpose of this discussion is to examine the course of bereavement following situations that produce massive collective stress and are caused by events that affect whole communities or subsets of a community.

COMMUNITY DISASTERS

The study of the psychological reaction to disaster takes on varying approaches depending on the conceptual biases of the researcher. These approaches can be characterized as: (a) individual reactions (impact of disaster on mental health status of individuals); (b) community reactions (impact of trauma on communities); and (c) systemic reactions (response to disaster within the context of the social system).

The type of disaster evaluated varies significantly and cannot be viewed as generalizable from one group to another. For example, a death caused by a critical incident (work or work-related disaster) may be responded to differently than a death from a community disaster because the survivors of the deceased killed in a critical incident may have had some prior knowledge of the risks associated with the job. A natural versus man-made disaster carries with it certain attributional implications that may or may not (depending on the cause) provide the individual with a target for directing his/her anger. Although it is not to be assumed that one type of disaster produces more disturbing or distressing symptomatology than another, each type of death generates certain confounding variables that complicate the interpretation of the data. Therefore, disaster-related research is wrought with conflicting interpretations of the same data, impeding the formulation of a model of disaster-related grief.

While it is important to address the conceptual issues outlined above, it is of particular import to summarize what is known about the impact of a disaster on the grief response of the survivor. To accomplish this task, we have established the following guidelines as a framework to guide the discussions that follow:

1. All data presented are based on disaster-related research that examined the disaster responses of relatives or loved ones of those killed in a community disaster or critical incident.
2. The responses by type of disaster are denoted as such when cited.
3. Given the purpose and format of this book, the information presented provides an examination of disaster-related symptomatology relative to changes in the functioning of the individual survivor. The context in which adaptation occurs is explored more fully in the assessment and treatment chapter of this section.
4. It is assumed that, generally speaking, nontraumatized populations do not exhibit symptomatology consistent with a diagnosis of Posttraumatic Stress Disorder. This assumption is supported by Helzer, Robins, and McEvoy's (1987) study of Post-traumatic Stress Disorder

symptomatology in the general population. They found that five men and 13 women per thousand had met the criteria for the disorder at some time in their lives. Therefore, this assumption is accepted as a point of comparison between exposed versus nonexposed groups.

There exists a minority of research that suggests that there is no psychological impairment produced by exposure to disaster-related trauma. Adler's (1943) study of psychiatric morbidity in survivors of the 1942 Coconut Grove fire disaster, which killed 491 patrons, found the percentage of respondents who had lost relatives or friends in the disaster was the same among those who developed psychiatric complications as it was in respondents whose personality did not manifest post-trauma changes. There are numerous methodological concerns with Adler's study in relation to his examination of bereavement (small sample size, relying on observation data only). This and other disaster-related studies included a wide range of survivors with varying degrees of exposure and loss relative to the disaster.

Conceptually, there can be no argument that the loss of a loved one or friend produces symptomatology consistent with that described in grief models (see Chapter 1). Furthermore, the exposure to disaster, via the loss of a relative or friend, fulfills Criteria A (experiencing of a qualifying event) of the DSM-IV criteria for a diagnosis of Post-traumatic Stress Disorder.

Therefore, it is logical to assume that some degree of change in the psychological functioning of the individual may occur, though certain factors may mitigate this impact. The following discussions outline the symptomatology produced by this type of trauma in keeping with the multidimensional symptom formulation format utilized throughout this section on traumatic death. It is proposed that the bereavement process is influenced by symptoms consistent with grief models and PTSD symptomatology. Research and case examples will be utilized to support this position. Furthermore, specific predictors of this type of grief are outlined as a means of implicating both empirical and clinical considerations.

The Immediate Response

The development of intervention services is dependent upon an accurate understanding of the survivor's specific needs in a temporal context. An exploration of Maslow's (1968) hierarchy of needs is useful in explaining this phenomenon. Maslow suggests a hierarchical continuum of needs, using the visual representation of a pyramid. At the base of the pyramid, he placed the deficiency needs such as food, water, and air, then safety needs such as shelter, followed by less immediate social needs such as the need to belong, the need to love and be loved, and the need to have self-esteem. At the apex of the pyramid lies what Maslow refers to as "the metaneeds," such as self-actualization. Fulfillment of self-actualization needs cannot be attained until all of the deficiency needs are met.

In many disasters, natural or man-made, there is significant property damage in addition to the loss of human life. Entire communities can be destroyed and many people are left homeless. Water and sewer systems can be damaged and food contamination and/or shortages are often consequences of the destruction. Disaster survivors cannot focus on the task of grieving when they are fighting to fulfill their most basic biological and safety needs. Therefore, it is helpful to explore some of the immediate psychological reactions to a disaster.

1. *Immobilization.* Survivor-victims report feelings of shock, numbness, denial, inability to concentrate, and feelings of unreality. Chad, a 32-year-old disaster survivor, who lost both parents in the Mount St. Helens volcanic disaster, described this time period in the following manner: "I felt as if I were walking around in a fog, like nothing was real. The emergency workers told me that my parents were dead and that everything was going to be O.K. At that time I was young and naive; I believed them." The first-order defenses such as projection, externalization, and denial allow the individual to defend against feelings of guilt and shame, block awareness of anger and fear, and protect against overwhelming emotion. While protracted utilization of this defensive complex can be maladaptive, initially it is purposeful.

2. *Multiple losses.* Surviving a disaster often means surviving the loss of loved ones, property, and possessions. The death toll may continue beyond the initial days of the crisis as some of the injured begin to die. The survivors may wonder when the death and dying will end. While the world watches the restoration processes in the aftermath of a disaster, the survivor-victim may feel as if the trauma is still occurring. Multiple losses can lead to "bereavement overload," severely taxing the individual's ability to cope.

3. *Helplessness.* Survivor-victims may feel overwhelmed by the destruction and loss and may become suicidal or develop the Learned Helplessness Syndrome (discussed further in later sections). Crisis intervention services should immediately assess the potential lethality of the survivor.

4. *Focus on survival.* The acquisition of adequate resources (food, shelter,

and clothing) becomes the focus of all the survivor's attention to the exclusion of all other concerns (funeral arrangements, social needs, academic concerns, emotional needs). The process of "biological" survival becomes an avoidance mechanism, protecting the survivor-victim from situations that could produce overwhelming emotions.

Post-disaster reactions often present as psychosocial problems prior to the manifestation or recognition of the long-term grief and trauma response. It is important that clinicians respond in a need-specific manner based on the survivor-victim's perception of need, regardless of the time since the disaster, since no exact time parameters for passage through any one stage or state of traumatic grief have been established.

Long-Term Survival

Survivor-victims may experience shame and guilt about their actions immediately following the disaster. Cognitive disturbance in the form of difficulty concentrating and memory impairment experienced by the survivor is often viewed as performance failure, and the individual, in retrospect, may regret the way he or she handled the disaster situation. Some may believe they could have taken action to save the lives of those around them if only they had acted more quickly or thought more clearly. This "survivor shame" leads to feelings of inadequacy, depression, and anxiety.

Titchener and Kapp (1976) studied the psychological impact on survivors of the 1972 Buffalo Creek flood in which 125 people were killed and 4,000 were left homeless. The issue of "survivor shame" is depicted in their case report of a flood survivor.

> One of the actual heros of Buffalo Creek, who had been extraordinarily effective in mobilizing and leading rescue efforts, was able to fend off depression and anxiety in the first four weeks after the flood while he worked relentlessly to help others. When he attempted to return to his former work, he was overwhelmed by anxiety and depression connected with feelings of inadequacy. He developed a phobia connected with his job, began drinking heavily, and became clinically depressed. (p. 297)

Despite this survivor's perceived "heroic efforts" to assist others during the immediate crisis period, he developed serious symptomatology as a result of his perception of "performance failure" in an impossible situation. The term *survivor shame* is used here instead of *survivor guilt* because initial feelings of guilt about surviving when others did not or responding inadequately to the disaster are internalized over time and become shame-based feelings of personal insignificance. Therefore, feelings about what the survivor-victim did or did not do become shame about who they are.

During the initial months following a natural disaster, survivors may report affective disturbances consistent with earlier descriptions of flooding and constriction (see Chapter 6). These responses consist of a range of symptoms from uncontrollable outbursts of anger, rage, sadness, and despair to a reported inability to feel any emotion. More severe symptoms are transient hallucinations and delusions, severe sleep disturbances and nightmares, intrusive images of deceased relatives and friends and of decomposed or damaged bodies, and obsessive attempts to protect themselves and their surviving loved ones from future harm. All survivor-victims struggle with issues of personal vulnerability (just as those impacted by murder or drunk driving) as they try to adapt to a world where there is no guaranteed protection against harm.

The magnitude of the events surrounding the death(s) produces a set of circumstances that may complicate the individual's interpretation of the meaning of death and view of him/herself in relation to the surrounding world. Disaster produces a multitude of losses: loss of life, loss of property and possessions, loss of relationships, and loss of self-esteem and self-worth. With each loss, there is a "dehumanization" of the individual, which occurs as the survivor-victim is exposed to events beyond his/her control. The following quotations from disaster survivors exemplify this phenomenon:

- "Every day we wondered what would happen next. It was like the world was out of control and nothing could stop it" (flood survivor).
- "It felt like there should be someone or something to appeal to for mercy, but there wasn't" (tornado survivor).
- "Nothing could fix the situation. Nothing could replace my husband or our home. There is no relief" (survivor of an apartment fire).

The acceptance of human vulnerability is a necessary part of the adaptive process. As the individual struggles with this task, resolution of attributional issues become key.

After a traumatic death caused by a human act (murder, drunk driving, etc.), attribution can be assigned to the perpetrator of the crime. In a natural disaster such as the Mount St. Helens volcanic eruption, Hurricane Agnes, the Topeka tornado of 1966, or other similar events, assigning blame becomes a more difficult task. The survivor-victim may ask questions such as "Am I to blame? If so, how do I forgive myself?" "Is God to blame? If so, is it acceptable to be angry or question God?"

Individual answers to these questions vary, but the significance of these answers is unquestioned. As individuals struggle with the emotional and spiritual implications of these answers, a strengthening of religious/spiritual convictions, a crisis of faith, or some combination of the two occurs. If the individual is not able to come to terms with this struggle, an "emotional vacuum" (Bard & Sangrey, 1986) is created, leaving the survivor with no target against which to direct his/her anger. The result is that the anger can be displaced, internalized, repressed, or misdirected, and acceptance of human vulnerability is impeded.

Much of the psychological presentation of the survivors is influenced by the struggle with these attributional issues. Society is programmed to understand the cause and effect relationship in almost all situations. Individuals need to understand why a tragedy occurs and then develop a strategy for future prevention. In many situations, this type of inquiry produces unsatisfactory answers, and this type of control may be impossible.

Following a disaster, survivor-victims may experience a series of adverse events that could be viewed as a second disaster, again depending on the nature of the original traumatic event. This second disaster may have as much predictive power with respect to the subsequent mental health functioning of the survivor as the original disaster. This phenomenon held true in the aftermath of the Buffalo Creek flood (as reported by Erikson, 1976) in that the entire community of 4,000 to 5,000 people was devastated as the displaced residents scattered, seeking shelter and safety. Therefore, not only was the Buffalo Creek community physically destroyed, so were the social support systems and resources of that community.

Research suggests that inadequate social support relates to the severity of symptoms related to PTSD and bereavement (Green, Grace, & Gleser, 1985; Kaniasty, Norris, & Murrell, 1990). A longitudinal study by Kaniasty et al. (1990) found that exposure to floods was linked with a subsequent decline in the perception of availability and the utilization of social support. While both wisdom of practice and empirical evidence support the notion that social support availability and utilization are significant variables to consider in the study of the process of bereavement, exactly how or why they are important is still debated. Lin, Simone, and Ensel (1979) suggest two possible ways in which social support works: (a) as a preventative factor protecting against the negative effects of normative stress, increasing the individual's ability to deal with more difficult stressful events when they arise, or (b) as a mediating factor in the life-events/illness equation once the event has occurred.

> Rebecca, a 62-year-old grandmother, entered treatment at the urging of her two grown children following the destruction of her home and community in a tornado. Although Rebecca's children state they "rallied around" their mother following the tragedy, offering physical, financial, and social support, Rebecca had declined their assistance, stating, "You have your own lives; there is no room for me." Rebecca became isolated and avoided activities that she had previously viewed as pleasurable.

In this case, the social support factor is further complicated by the individual's cognitive appraisal of support. In order to assess an individual's social resources and the significance of these supporting structures on the bereavement process, one must evaluate the individual's perception of his/her social network and the availability of someone viewed as a reliable confidant. Both practice and research (Bromet & Dunn, 1981; Green et al., 1985; Shore, Tatum, & Volmer, 1986) support the premise that environmental and family system interactions are complex determinants of mental health outcomes. Analyzing an individual's social interactions or transactions utilizes an external frame of reference, a distinction often overlooked by social science research.

Destruction of the supportive resources in a community (as with the Buffalo Creek flood) can impact the mitigation of post-trauma stress via social support, regardless of the social support model espoused. Social involvement, however, has been found to differentially mediate the effect of disaster exposure on the mental health of male and female victims (Solomon, Smith, Robins, & Fischbach, 1987). Social demands may play a crucial role in the mediation of post-trauma stress. For example, excellent spousal support may attenuate male symptomatology, while its presence can be associated with an exacerbation of symptoms in females. These results suggest the importance of considering the positive and negative consequences of social involvement because, for women, very strong social ties may become more burdensome than supportive after a disaster.

One differentiating characteristic of a community disaster from other types of traumas resulting in fatalities is the degree of loss produced by the event. For example, most murders or drunk driving fatalities produced one or multiple victims. Community disasters may cause the loss of life, but they can produce other losses as well. Research on survivors of the Buffalo Creek flood (Gleser, Green, & Winget, 1981) and the Beverly Hills Supper Club fire (Green et al., 1985) illustrates this point. Clinical practice with survivors of these types of disasters, as well as the research, supports the thesis that the degree of loss (from possessions to immediate family) and overall functioning are significantly related. Specifically, the greater the degree of loss, the greater the functional impairment.

One reason for this relates back to the previous discussion regarding the nature of the disaster, the impact on the community, and the importance of social support. The Beverly Hills Supper Club fire killed more people than the Buffalo Creek flood, but the impact on the overall community was less. In short, although more lives were lost, the disaster was somewhat contained (did not affect the entire community), and the potential for recurrence was low. Therefore, survivors were not displaced, so that community and supportive resources remained intact.

This situation can be contrasted to the 1980 Mount St. Helens volcanic eruption, which claimed the lives of 50 people. The potential for subsequent eruption and flooding provided an ongoing, long-term threat to the survivors, thus complicating the adaptive process for a prolonged period of time. Research designed to study the impact of this disaster on the bereaved population also noted a high correlation between the degree of loss and subsequent psychiatric morbidity (Shore et al., 1986). One year after the eruption, these researchers found onset rates of single-episode depression, generalized anxiety disorder, and Post-traumatic Stress Disorder 11 to 12 times higher than those observed in the control community. Therefore, the greater the loss suffered due to the disaster, the greater the prevalence and duration of psychiatric morbidity.

In summation, the following factors should be considered in the assessment of survivors of disasters:

1. Evaluate the survivors' perception of their role performance in the disaster. Differentiate between shame and guilt issues.
2. Assess the status of resources: financial, physical, and social.
3. Determine the individual's cognitive appraisal of the availability of social support.
4. Note the degree of loss.
5. Assess the extent of the distress, considering disturbances such as mood disorders and anxiety disorders in addition to grief symptomatology.

6. Be aware of intrapersonal struggles with attributional issues and the extent to which these conflicts have defined the individuals' perception of themselves and their world.

Although all of these issues may not manifest in every disaster survivor, an initial and ongoing evaluation of these factors is necessary for accurate assessment and treatment.

Duration of the Traumatic Grief Response

One of the most significant differences in the grief process following a traumatic death versus death by natural causes is the duration of symptomatology. Generally speaking, grief resolution is more rapid after a death by natural causes than after a traumatic death. One partial explanation for this difference is the lack of anticipatory grieving inherent in the traumatic grief process. Even so, this factor does not offer sufficient explanation for the within-group and between-group variances in grief responses across all modes of death. It is suggested that the mode of death and the subsequent implications of a traumatic death are the most important (though not the only) variables to consider in determining the duration of the traumatic grief response.

Research regarding the duration of post-disaster symptomatology is still somewhat preliminary and ambiguous in nature. Some researchers suggest that the pathology after a natural disaster such as a volcano, flood, or tornado persists as long as three years, though most symptoms begin to abate by about 16 months (Bravo, Rubio-Stipec, Canino, Woodbury, & Ribera, 1990; Krause, 1987; Shore et al., 1986; Steinglass & Gerrity, 1990). Research on man-made disasters such as fires or bombings suggests that symptomatology may persist as long as 14 years following a disaster (Green et al., 1985). These researchers found an increase in distress and hostility two years following the disaster. Clinical, empirical, and anecdotal information supports the usual duration of symptomatology well beyond the parameters generally accepted for uncomplicated bereavement. In fact, a descriptive study of 22 clinical cases evaluated by the authors of this book reveal 82% report experiencing grief and/or PTSD symptomatology beyond the two-year anniversary of the disaster.

While no clear explanation for this phenomenon is accepted, this finding does raise the possibility that the initial periods of emotional constriction presented as shock, denial, and numbness may be prolonged (therefore delaying the movement through the process of grief), and affective acknowledgment may be exacerbated by unstable conditions and the destruction of resources and networks.

Multidimensional Symptom Formulation

Affective Responses

Previous discussions of traumatic affective grief-related symptomatology reveal a tendency toward intrapsychic struggles to regulate the often overwhelming levels of affect produced by the traumatic stimuli. The emotional acknowledgment of the multiple losses experienced in a natural or man-made disaster represents a necessary part of traumatic grief resolution. A disaster-induced bereavement is consistent with earlier depictions of traumatic grief with respect to the affective response of the individual. Affective symptomatology includes sadness, anger, crying spells, irritability, numbness, explosive defensive reactions against perceived attacks on the self, and constricted affective states. The subjective experience of emotion often manifests as flat, labile, blunted, restricted, inappropriate, or broad in those struggling with overwhelming levels of emotion.

It is important to assess (a) the type of affectual (external) response exhibited, as an indication of the pervasive and sustained mood that is experienced internally, and (b) the capacity of the individual to tolerate overwhelming levels of emotions and the ego resources available for the task of adaptation.

Cognitive Responses

Assessing the level of mood disturbance and the affective manifestations of a disaster-induced grief response is essential, as these can impact the cognitive functioning of the survivor-victim. Research and case study reveal that the additive demands of trauma and grief produce cognitive symptomatology consistent with both models. There is evidence of lack of concentration, memory loss, ruminations and worry, guilt, intrusive thoughts, fear and worry about the possibility of another disaster, and struggles with the proper assignment of accountability. Since cognition is an ego function closely related to judgment, impairment in cognitive functioning is often accompanied by impaired judgment. Poor judgment or a loss of faith in one's ability to accurately judge a person or situation can manifest in various negative ways, further exacerbating the cognitive disturbance by undermining the self-confidence of the mourner.

Behavioral Responses

Both mood and cognitions impact the behavioral responses of the survivor-victim. These responses span the continuum from avoidance of disaster-related stimuli, social isolation, and withdrawal to an increase of aggressive behavior as a means of dealing with the anger, rage, and terror induced by the disaster. The acting out brings about temporary partial relief of inner tension. The individual attains this relief by reacting to a present situation as if it were the original trauma that produced the drive or impulse.

Despite the immediate relief achieved by acting out, the consequence of this behavior is generally negative and can prove destructive to healthy aspects of the individual's life (e.g., marriage, job, social group). Avoidance behaviors that successfully, if only temporarily, alleviate the source of aversive stimuli are reinforced and maintained. While some of these behaviors may be natural and healthy defensive strategies initially, they can become maladaptive with time, posing significant challenges to traumatic grief resolution.

Physiological Responses

Individuals who are unable to tolerate the often overwhelming emotions produced by disaster-related grief may develop a somatization disorder characterized by multiple physical complaints of unknown etiology. More and more researchers and scientists are finding links, however, between trauma and physiological changes in the human body (see Chapter 5). Some of these responses include physical symptoms of arousal such as trembling, exaggerated startle response, hypervigilance, psychomotor retardation or agitation, sleep and appetite disturbance, changes in immune system and cardiac system functioning, and the physiological reexperiencing of the disaster produced by seemingly benign stimuli.

These physiological responses can lead to behavioral disturbances (substance abuse, avoidance of people and places that represent the disaster, poor job performance, social isolation) as the individual tries to control or hide these physical manifestations of traumatic grief. Table 8.1 summarizes this multidimensional symptom formulation.

Traumatic Grief and Personality Functioning

Previous discussions have focused on the Axis I disorders that represent a class of diagnostic information pertinent to clinical syndromes. Empirical study of the impact of trauma on the psychological functioning of the survivor-victims generally pertains to the exploration of symptomatology consistent with an Axis I diagnosis. As exploration of the additive influence of grief and trauma progresses, a number of significant factors

TABLE 8.1
**Multidimensional Symptom Formulation for Community
Disaster-Induced Bereavement**

Affective	Cognitive	Behavioral	Physiological
Emotional constriction	Decreased or difficulty with concentration	Obsessive attempts to protect self or others	Sleep disturbance
Emotional flooding	Memory impairment	Social withdrawal/ isolation	Appetite disturbance
Survivor shame	Intrusive images	Avoidance of disaster site or disaster-related stimuli	Trembling
Guilt	Rumination		Physiological arousal
Anger/rage	Loss of interest	Acting out	Physiological reexperiencing
Fear	Struggles with assignment of accountability	Substance abuse	Somatization
Sadness/ depression		Impaired occupational, academic, and social functioning	
Numbness	Worry about another disaster	Decreased task involvement	
Feelings of personal insignificance	Impaired judgment	Disruption of daily routines	
Anxiety			
Irritability			
Crying spells			

emerge that complicate the adaptation process (e.g., survivor-shame, dehumanization, loss of self-esteem, issues regarding the assignment of proper accountability). While the data outlining the duration of the traumatic grief response are preliminary in nature, there is evidence that the mode of death and the circumstances (social and environmental) the survivor-victim must deal with may have a lasting impact upon the personality functioning of the individual. The importance of an accurate Axis classification has treatment and prognostic significance.

While much of the empirical work on community disasters uncovered psychiatric morbidity in the form of clinical syndromes, one must contemplate the overall impact of this disturbance on the individual's personality, given the often prolonged nature of the disturbance. It seems the loss of control and vulnerability imposed by random destruction and loss produced by the disaster may change the way the individual views himself and his world. Some may argue that these changes may cause changes in personality functioning.

Exposure to a disaster and the process of grief thereafter does not mandate the manifestation of pathology. While the disaster can produce some disabling symptoms such as anxiety and depression, in addition to the grief symptomatology produced by the loss(es), the course of bereavement is dependent upon a number of endogenous and exogenous variables unique to the individual mourner. These factors are explored further in the following discussions.

Variables Impacting the Traumatic Grief Reaction Following a Disaster

The DSM-IV (APA, 1994) describes uncomplicated bereavement as the "normal" reaction to the death of a loved one that "rarely occurs after the first two or three months" (p. 684). The previous discussions describe how the process of grief after a traumatic, disaster-related death is always complicated, intense, and enduring. The factors impacting the course of bereavement are psychologically, socially, and culturally oriented and are specific to the mode of death.

Learned Helplessness

Many individuals may be predisposed to develop post-disaster psychiatric disorders due to past experiences with trauma or death that, if unresolved, confound the bereavement process. Exploration of the development and course of the Learned Helplessness Syndrome is useful in illustrating the impact of endogenous variables on the resolution of traumatic grief.

Seligman and Maier (1968) performed the classic studies on vulnerability utilizing canine subjects. Their purpose was to create a situation analogous to human trauma. With repeated failure at attempted trials to overcome the adverse situation presented, Seligman and Maier noticed that the dogs acquired a loss of motivation, had a decreased level of interaction with the other dogs and with the experimenters, and became withdrawn from their environment. Based on this experience, they developed the hypothesis that frequent experience with a lack of contingency between response and outcome will lead the organism to assume that it is helpless.

When the experimenters removed the obstacles from the avoidance cage and rang the buzzer, they observed that despite the passage of time, and even with forceful reexposure (by dragging the dogs across the cage to demonstrate they would not be shocked), many of the canine subjects refused to cross the cage again. Ingram (1986) offers an explanation for this type of reaction in humans when he suggests that individuals selectively ignore information that contradicts the schemas already in place. In this way, the tendency toward help-lessness is self-perpetuated.

Flannery (1987) expounded on the work of Seligman and Maier, gener-alizing their findings to humans by proposing five common themes for individuals with learned helplessness: (a) perception of a lack of control over one's life; (b) failure to undertake any task involvement; (c) disrup-tion in daily routines; (d) high intake of dietary stimulants; and (e) avoidance or low utilization of social support.

It is apparent that the factors described by Flannery are inherent to disaster by nature of the event. The loss of control experienced by the survivor-victim is exacerbated by the chaos created by the disaster. Not only has a loved one been killed in the disaster, there may be destruction of the individual's home or community, personal injury, or the involve-ment of "outsiders" in the restoration effort. All these factors lead to a loss of control, disruption of daily routines, and changes in social net-works. Still, not everyone exposed to a disaster develops the Learned Helplessness Syndrome. Research and practice indicate there are other variables specific to the disaster itself that can influence the course of bereavement and the adaptive process.

Inoculation Hypothesis

While unresolved issues related to past trauma may manifest in the development of the Learned Helplessness Syndrome, successful experi-ences in coping with trauma may be advantageous to the survivor-victim. The study by Norris and Murrell (1988) of 234 older adult survivors of the southeastern Kentucky flood provided support for the "inoculation hypothesis" and other conceptualizations that emphasize the advan-tages of prior experience with the current stressor in healthy adaptation. When comparing victims with previous flood experience to those who were "newly" exposed to this type of disaster, they found significant differences in the development of post-disaster psychiatric disturbance. The previously exposed victims exhibited no trait anxiety or weather-specific distress, while the "newly" exposed group demonstrated mod-est effects in both areas.

Level of Exposure

The proximity of the survivor-victim at the time of the disaster and the type of loss(es) incurred are of particular significance because these variables relate to the amount of disaster exposure experienced. Conceptually, the higher the level of exposure to the disaster, the more material the survivor has to ruminate about and the greater the possibility of intrusive or disturbing images. Many clients report considerable ongoing distress about the condition of the bodies they encountered and the scenes of destruction they witnessed. The threat of future harm may also exist and exacerbate post-trauma grief symptoms.

Threat of Future Harm

The authors' study of the clinical response of disaster survivors produces evidence of efforts to prevent future harm by avoidance of situations similar to the initial disaster. Although the chances of revictimization by another disaster are slim, the threat of a recurrence or the threat imposed by the unpredictability of the future is often great enough to significantly alter the survivor's behavior in a maladaptive manner. In the case of a natural disaster such as the Mount St. Helens eruption or the southeastern Kentucky floods, the risk was not alleviated at the time of the initial disaster. The survivor-victims in both of these incidents faced the threat of another eruption or flood while experiencing the harm produced by the destruction of the community (loss of safety, unsanitary living conditions, illness, financial loss, etc.). The potential for subsequent harm gives a dual aspect to the disaster and poses an ongoing long-term threat to the mental health of the survivor-victims.

The Evacuation Process

The process of evacuating individuals from a disaster or impending disaster can be as traumatic as the disaster itself. Family members who were involved in and survived the Buffalo Creek flood described the visual horror associated with stepping over body parts and witnessing the drowning of their relatives and friends trying to escape the flood site. While rescue workers attempted to save those who could be saved, those who survived suffered survivor guilt, fearing they had evacuated too soon or could have somehow saved the deceased by staying at the disaster site. The inherent chaos in a disaster produces a situation analogous to the course of bereavement. The survivor feels out of control, focused on survival, and may use primitive defenses to survive (sacrificing others for his/her own survival). Resolution of the grief process becomes dependent upon resolving the shame and guilt associated with these acts.

Kilijanek and Drabek (1979) studied the impact on the mental health status of the elderly of the 1966 tornado in Topeka, Kansas, that killed 17, injured 550, and left 1,600 families homeless. They found that the mobility of the subjects was of particular significance in the subsequent course of adaptation. Physical impairment or the limitations to mobility caused by age or injury may add to the overall stress produced in the evacuation stage and the adaptive process thereafter.

CRITICAL INCIDENTS

Work or work-related disasters or critical incidents describe a type of trauma induced by a single-victim or a multicasualty disaster. The grief response to this type of disaster is multidimensional and similar in nature to other types of disaster-induced bereavement. There are, however, certain variables specific to this mode of death that impact the course of bereavement.

Workers who deal regularly with critical incidents, along with their family and friends, undergo a type of "emotional inoculation" to the impact of disaster and are generally familiar with the policies and procedures developed to handle pre- and post-disaster situations. The emotional and behavioral rehearsal that employees and their families go through as part of a disaster-preparedness training may equip them with the skills they need for survival. Unfortunately, other employers and employees fail to acknowledge the possibility of a critical incident occurring, leaving workers and their families unprepared for the tragedy when it occurs.

The knowledge of risk, however slight, sets up a cause-effect relationship between the nature of the work and the ensuing disaster that may impact the survivor's perception of personal vulnerability. If the survivor-victim can find a satisfactory cause for the disaster, than preservation of the myth of invulnerability becomes possible. The survivor-victim may decide that better planning, improved decision making, or avoidance of potentially dangerous situations will protect him/her from future harm. Therefore, order and control are restored and loss of esteem is minimized. On the other hand, those who recognize the risk and understand the safety processes necessary for proper risk reduction may struggle with intense levels of rage and anger at those they feel could have or should have prevented the tragedy.

Cumulative trauma becomes an essential factor for those who are repeatedly exposed to work-site disasters. Workers and their families may react to the effects of cumulative trauma versus the isolated incident.

This sets up a "traumatic overload" situation that parallels "bereavement overload," severely taxing the survivor-victims' emotional resources. In order to deal with the overwhelming levels of affect caused by attributional or cumulative trauma issues, many survivor-victims focus their anger on the judicial system.

Research involving the legal response of survivor-victims of critical incident disasters shows a tendency toward litigation in the aftermath of the tragedy, demonstrating a high need to seek revenge and assign culpability for the deaths or injuries that occurred (Badenhorst & Van Schalkwyk, 1992). If survivor-victims are unable to focus their anger on an individual or a group, the employer is often targeted for redress. In their research on the post-disaster response of the survivors of a South African mine explosion that killed 52 workers, they found that early detection of PTSD and other disaster effects, as well as prompt intervention, produced decreases in litigation among the recipients of these services.

Decreased litigation among employees and families who received employer-based interventions suggests that these survivors may feel the employers are concerned with the emotional recovery of survivors, which in turn increases their loyalty to the company. For those who pursue legal recourse, preoccupation with civil or criminal proceedings serves as an avoidance mechanism, often preventing affective acknowledgment of the loss(es). Since the civil and criminal systems are inundated with cases, delays of one to four years or more are not uncommon. For many, resolution of grief cannot be achieved until adjudication of the case is completed.

The majority of critical-incident research focuses on the psychological response of the surviving workforce or the debriefing/recovery process. There is a paucity of research examining the traumatic grief process following a critical incident. It is helpful, however, to delineate some of the situation-specific trauma reactions that may permeate the bereavement process. These reactions (in addition to those already mentioned in Table 8.1) are in Table 8.2 (Badenhorst & Van Schalkwyk, 1992; Frolkey, 1992; Hillenburg & Wolf, 1988; Singleton & Teahan, 1978).

CONCLUSION

This chapter provides an overview of the empirical and clinical explorations of the post-disaster traumatic grief response. The process of grief is impacted by the situational variables associated with the manner of dying and the characteristics inherent to the individual survivor. Since

TABLE 8.2
Multidimensional Symptom Format for Critical-Incident Trauma Reactions

Affective	Cognitive	Behavioral	Physiological
Sudden mood changes	Decreased concentration	Erratic work or social involvement	Somatization
Irritability	Memory impairment	Substance abuse	Changes in appetite
Unwarranted grievances	Difficulty following complicated instructions	Impairment of occupational, academic, social functioning	Changes in sleep patterns
Detachment from similarly affected families/friends	Poor judgment and decision making	Avoidance of the disaster site or related stimuli	Physiological reexperiencing
Rage/anger	Ruminations	Increased involvement in judicial system	Physiological arousal
Denial/shock	Intrusive images	Engaging in dangerous behavior (to self or others)	

psychological symptoms and recovery issues can be diverse across groups, treatment flexibility is crucial. The following chapter presents an overview of assessment and treatment goals and methods for dealing with victims of all types of traumatic grief. Situation-specific examples are given as a means of illustrating the special issues unique to the mode of death.

9

The Treatment of
Traumatic Grief

This chapter will present assessment and treatment methods applicable to survivor-victims who have lost a loved one in a traumatic manner. A generalized approach to dealing with all types of traumatic grief processes is established, though situation-specific examples are provided to guide the reader through the unique emotional, cognitive, behavioral, and physiological recovery processes relative to the particular mode of death.

Whether the goal of therapy is psychosocial change or crisis stabilization, it requires introspection and increased levels of self-awareness for survivor-victims after the traumatic death of a loved one. For clinicians dealing with traumatized clients, the process of assessing the capacities and survival skills of the survivor-victim is essential. These individuals are faced with the challenge of transforming their social and physical environments in a manner that provides for systemic equilibrium.

Social scientists wrestle with ideological conflicts over issues regarding the form, process, and function of change. Technically, these discussions center around the notion of human plasticity or the psychological capacity of an individual to change and to adapt to adversity. How and why change and adaptation occur varies, depending on many factors, including the theoretical perspective espoused. While it is not the intent of this chapter to propose a purist approach to practice, the techniques and methods presented assume a constructivist perspective in that: (a) psychological distress after a traumatic event is a natural expression of an individual's current personal reality; and (b) this distress is a necessary element in the reorganization and adaptation process. It is also assumed that most individuals possess the emotional resources necessary for healthy adaptation, though some encounter more difficulty than others. Scarr (1982) understood this when writing,

> Human beings are made of neither glass that breaks in the slightest ill wind nor of steel that stands defiantly in the face of devastating hurricanes. Rather . . . humans bend with environmental pressures, resume their shapes when the pressures are relieved, and are unlikely to be permanently misshapen by transient experiences. When bad environments are improved, people's adaptation improve. Human beings are resilient to the advantages their environments provide. Even adults are capable of improved adaptations through learning, although any individual's improvement depends on that person's responsiveness to learning opportunities. (p. 853)

Human capacity for change is considerable, though limited by the individual who must acquire healthy adaptative processes from trial-and-error efforts to regain dynamic equilibrium. Processes underlying human change and adaptation are nonlinear and complex, preventing absolute predictions of the course of any adaptive process. Clinicians are required to continually reassess the progress and course of therapeutic endeavors and must learn to listen to the guideposts provided by their clients.

The following information is not presented as the "absolute truth" nor a "guarantee" for successful practice with traumatized individuals. The techniques and methods should be utilized in an approach that is individualized and personal. There are no exact time parameters for completion of the bereavement process, so it is incumbent on the individual practitioner to collaboratively set realistic goals with their clients based on the individual's specific capacities and emotional resources.

INTERVENTION STRATEGIES

There are three phases of the intervention process: (a) initial evaluation and debriefing; (b) assessment and treatment; and (c) maintenance and support. Because trauma induces a pervasive disruption of the self, therapeutic content will focus on different levels of personality: intrapersonal, interpersonal, individual-social conflicts, and actualization/fulfillment issues.

Recovery from traumatic grief requires interventions that focus on each level of personality functioning. It is important that the therapist assess the level of personality affected so as to most appropriately deter-mine the mode of intervention (individual, conjoint, family).

Evaluation and Debriefing

This phase of the intervention process occurs immediately following the traumatic event and focuses on crisis intervention and stabilization of the individual's emotional, social, and physical environment.

As discussed earlier in this chapter, the survivor-victim's immediate needs following a traumatic event center around physical and emotional survival. Transtheoretical therapy appreciates the validity of all levels of problems—intrapersonal, interpersonal, socioenvironmental, etc. An eclectic approach generally intervenes initially at the symptom/situation level to produce the most immediate and conscious change. Clinicians should focus on stabilization of the individual's emotional, physical, and social situation and the symptoms of distress imposed by these social and environmental pressures. Specifically, the following intervention strategies are suggested:

1. Do not initially challenge the client's use of first-order defenses. Sup-port, validation, and normalization of the client's reaction to the trau-matic loss is appropriate.
2. Prepare the client for multiple losses. Do not discount the impact of subsequent losses of role, status, relationships, other deaths, self-esteem, etc. Encourage ventilation and offer supportive types of ther-apy at this time. Slowly begin to educate clients as to what they can expect in the coming months, and seek to dispel any unrealistic expectation about the grief process. The clinician should exercise cau-tion against overwhelming clients with too much information, as their emotional and cognitive capacities may be preoccupied by the process of self-preservation.

   The initial days and weeks may be accompanied by multiple crises as the individual struggles to cope with the aftermath of the trauma. The therapist should distinguish between sudden loss (the initial death) and gradual loss (the subsequent losses that occur over a period of time). Clients may overlook the significance of gradual loss on the grief process by focusing their recovery on a single episode of loss as opposed to the progression of losses imposed by the trauma.
3. Screen for critical indicators. Traumatized individuals may experience helplessness and hopelessness so extreme that they may become suicidal or homicidal. While suicidal or homicidal ideation is not un-

common, those with a specific plan, a history of previous attempts, or current substance abuse will require more intensive intervention initially.

4. Address the physical and financial aspects of the loss. Depending upon the type of trauma experienced, survivor-victims are faced with basic deficiency needs that must be met before they can address their psychological needs. The clinician should provide a list of resources (food, shelter, clothing, financial assistance, day care) to assist them in dealing with the socioenvironmental impact of the trauma.

For victims of crime, the Crime Victim's Compensation Fund is available in most states to assist crime victims with funeral arrangements, loss of wages, psychotherapy services, medical services and supplies. For victims of community disasters, the Red Cross is generally called upon to coordinate the relief efforts. In critical incidents, the company's Employee Assistance Program is generally equipped to handle Critical Incident Debriefings. The Appendix provides a resource list of available stabilization, intervention, and support services.

Immediate post-trauma reactions often present as psychosocial problems prior to the manifestation or recognition of the long-term grief and trauma implications. It is important that clinicians respond in a need-specific manner based on the survivor-victims' perception of need, regardless of the time since the disaster, since no specific time parameters for passage through any one stage or state of traumatic grief have been established.

As the client learns to adapt to the immediate needs produced by the trauma, the client and the therapist may realize the need for more psychologically focused intervention to deal with the ongoing, long-term impact of the traumatic loss. To adequately determine the specific needs and strengths of the individual, a thorough assessment should be performed.

Assessment

A multidimensional assessment taps into the many dimensions of the individual's life: emotional, social, and environmental. To adequately guide the assessment process, Table 9.1 illustrates the targets of assessment for the traumatized, grieving client.

Methods utilized to gather the above-mentioned material include clinical interviews, psychometric testing, collateral reports, and observation. The use of a particular assessment tool is dependent upon the personal

TABLE 9.1
Targets of Assessment

Dimension	Client	Family	Social
Affective	Mood, affect History of affective disturbance Feelings about the death, self, God, losses, therapy	Feelings about the deceased Nature of the emotional bonds in the family Feelings of the family about the trauma/grief Emotional support available Affective nature of the family	Sentiment of culture *re* trauma, death, grief, and treatment Available support
Cognitive	Cognitive style Intelligence Education Attitudes and expectations Philosophy of life Thought content Thought process Perceived meaning of trauma/death Knowledge of trauma/grief Memory of event	Understanding of trauma/grief Attitudes and expectations Intellectual resources Philosophy of life Perceived meaning of trauma	Sophistication of culture Current knowledge Cultural attitudes
Behavioral	Social interaction Past treatment utilization Substance abuse Isolating behavior Activity level or involvement Avoidance behavior	Participation in therapy Reinforcement contingencies utilized by family Interactive patterns Substance abuse	Customs regarding symptom reporting/ treatment seeking Interactive patterns Restoration activity Availability
Physiological or Physical	Age, sex, race Health status Physiological symptoms of arousal Somatization patterns Medications Appearance Physical disturbance	Genetic influence Status of family dwelling Family characteristics Size of family Economic resources Health status	Resource availability Networks Health hazards Community destruction Financial resources available

preference of the therapist, though it is suggested that assessments be multidimensional in nature and comprehensive enough to tap the various dimensions in an individual's life. A few of these approaches are outlined here as a brief overview of available assessment methods.

Psychometric Measures

Several measures have been developed that address some of the issues neglected by the SCID. These can be used in conjunction with the clinical interview.

The Mississippi PTSD scales (M-PTSD) were developed by Keane, Caddell, and Taylor (1988) for administration to military and civilian persons who had experienced a trauma. These scales consist of 39 items designed to indicate the severity of the disorder. The authors suggest a cutoff score of 107, with higher ratings indicating more severe cases. Kulka et al. (1990) suggest that respondents who score 107 or higher represent the treatment-seeking population and suggest 89 as a more appropriate cutoff. Using this cutoff score, reliability and validity ratings for all three subscales (combat veterans, spouses, and civilians) are high, and there seems to be a consensus in the literature that 89 is the most acceptable cutoff score.

The Impact of Events (IES) scale was designed by Horowitz et al. (1979) and measures the level of traumatic stress on two dimensions: intrusive symptomatology and avoidance symptomatology. The 15-item measure contains these two subscales: Intrusive scale (items 1–7) and Avoidance scale (items 8–15). This measure is especially sensitive to cases in which a chronicity of symptomatology is evident. Test-retest and split-half reliability ratings are in the high .80s. Tests to determine validity ratings demonstrate a strong correlation between the validity of the IES and scores on the Mississippi scales.

Keane, Malloy, and Fairbanks (1984) recognized the need to have a PTSD subscale added to the MMPI. This subscale cannot be integrated into the MMPI as a valid subscale at this time, as false positives and negatives are high. The authors suggest utilization of the subscale as a supplement to the clinical evaluation, but do not advise the abstraction of the 40 items from the MMPI as a sole measure of PTSD. They feel that the subscale, in final form, will have good sensitivity and specificity.

It is important to note that often PTSD symptoms are misdiagnosed due to the inadequacy of the MMPI to measure this disorder. There is evidence throughout the literature (Kulka et al., 1990; Pynoos & Spencer, 1985) of studies that correlate PTSD symptomatology with clinical disturbances measured by the clinical scales of the MMPI. It is evident from these findings that there is a definite possibility of misdiagnosis when one is utilizing scales that do not specifically tap the PTSD dimension.

Differential Diagnosis

There are some variants of PTSD overlooked by the standard diagnostic classifications that should be considered. Most of these variations follow the Polythetic Criteria Rule (possessing some symptoms from Criteria B, C, and D of the DSM-IV classification of PTSD).

The first variation is called the B-D alcohol/drug type. In this posttrauma manifestation, the subject displays symptoms that meet the B and D criteria for the disorder, but experience no numbing or avoidance symptomatology. In these trauma survivors, alcohol or drug abuse is used as an external means of avoiding flashbacks. These individuals tend to self-medicate, demonstrating an unwillingness or inability to access internal coping mechanisms. Individuals suffering from the B-D Alcohol variant of this disorder will usually meet the criteria for Substance Abuse or Dependency and are often among the most severely traumatized populations.

Severely traumatized children may exhibit additional symptomatology not included in the DSM-IV. These difficulties include attachment difficulties and nonspecific disorders such as hyperactivity and restlessness. Additionally, there is an increased occurrence of neurotic manifestations such as bed-wetting and regression in developmental milestones (thumb sucking, etc.).

An Acute Stress Disorder diagnosis can be made if dissociative symptomatology was present for at least two days, but no longer than four weeks. These symptoms include, numbing, detachment, absence of emotional responsiveness, reduction of awareness, derealization, depersonalization, or dissociative amnesia. At least one symptom from each PTSD symptom cluster must be present. The inclusion of this disorder in the DSM-IV addresses many of the "subclinical" cases of PTSD that were misdiagnosed because there wasn't sufficient symptomatology to qualify for an APA-sanctioned diagnosis, but appear closely related to the traumatic grief experience.

To further assist in the development of a typology of traumatic grief, a distinction regarding predominate symptomatology could be classified. For example, a Type C avoidance type would designate a grieving individual who may meet all the criteria for PTSD but has a prevalence of avoidance symptomatology (e.g., denial, withdrawal, memory impairment, or diminished interest). A typology of this type facilitates communication and understanding between clinicians and provides for a certain diagnostic specificity that could have important research implications.

Currently, PTSD is classified as an anxiety disorder. Given the complication of traumatic grief, there are some significant diagnostic challenges that arise due to the overlapping of symptoms that are indicative of other disorders (e.g., sleep disorders, phobias, depression, etc.). Some of the sleep disturbance and nervousness associated with a trauma survivor may indicate a co-occurrence of a generalized anxiety disorder. The occurrence of a trauma makes the PTSD diagnosis primary. Obsessive-compulsive disorder is also listed as an anxiety disorder and may have common symptomatology with PTSD. Intrusiveness of thought and ruminations are inherent in both disorders, but the OCD diagnosis should be made only if the repetitive behavior, such as checking or hand washing, is evident.

There is a high co-occurrence of PTSD and phobic disorders. It is suggested that a history of phobic disorders may be linked to the development of PTSD due to the tendency toward physiological tension inherent in the phobia patient. This overtension is indicative of the presence of insufficient coping strategies in the individual, which in turn may lead to maladaptive post-trauma reactions.

There is also evidence of a co-occurrence of PTSD, grief symptomatology, and major depressive disorders. Again, the co-occurrence of trauma would indicate the depressive disorder as secondary. For severe or chronic cases of PTSD, there will often be a co-occurrence of dysthymia and PTSD. Since all grief associated with a traumatic death is complicated, the grief may present as a mood disorder. While the co-occurrence of grief, PTSD, and a mood disorder is certainly possible, it is imperative that the clinician be attentive to the nature of the grief response after a traumatic death so as not to respond inappropriately to the presenting symptomatology.

Interventions

Due to the co-occurrence of various symptomatology, the use of medications to treat post-traumatic grief reactions is controversial. Some clinicians may feel it is counterintuitive to use pharmacological approaches to deal with a reactive disorder. Tricyclic antidepressants, MAO inhibitors, and carbamazepine tend to have greater efficacy in treating the intrusion and hyperarousal states as opposed to the numbing and avoidance symptomatology, and the research shows that imipramine and phenelzine alleviate the intrusive symptoms of PTSD among Vietnam veterans.

In any case, where symptomatology has produced marked functional impairment, a medication consultation is certainly warranted. In these cases, pharmacological interventions may make the process of psychotherapy more productive by removing the tendency to deny and repress distressing recollections and by facilitating the memory integration process. However, the use of medications, while promising in some cases, may actually mask symptoms and complicate the grieving process; therefore, they should be used sparingly.

Too often, methods designed to help a mourner actually complicate or impede the process. Family and friends of murder victims report frustration and despair at the lack of technologically sound, quality resources available. In the experience of the senior author, the bereaved came to seek treatment after various unsuccessful attempts to acquire quality therapeutic services. This was for a number of reasons: (1) limited number of therapists who have training or experience with this population; (2) therapists who apply the traditional models of grief to the therapeutic process, often invalidating the more intense symptomatolgy of these mourners; and (3) limited number of support or community resources, or resources that are inappropriate due to the characteristics of the group. Community resources are sometimes limited or may not be appropriate venues for some. Support groups, for example, can help or hinder grief work depending upon the composition, agenda, and purpose of the group. Some mourners actually become "stuck" at a particular point in the grief process due to overinvolvement in a particular case or cause. Some may need to leave a group in order to progress. Still others seek out support or advocacy groups as a means of working through feelings of anger, hopelessness, and frustration. The support found in these settings may not be replicated by outside sources. Therapists should critically examine their own competency when working with certain clients, as well as the competency of referral sources, to determine if they have the training and skills necessary to provide quality services to this special population. What may be appropriate at one stage may need to be reevaluated periodically during the course of treatment.

What Clients Want

A survey conducted by the senior author of family and friends who had suffered the loss of a loved one in a traumatic event uncovered the following comments about what the bereaved felt was the most or least beneficial component of the therapeutic process.

- "I just wanted to know what to expect. I can handle anything if I can prepare for it."
- "I needed to know if I was going crazy or not. I was sure I was—my therapist gave me a book on grief that wasn't me. It didn't fit."
- "My therapist let me tell the story over and over. I don't know why that was helpful—I just needed to try and understand."
- "I needed some guidance—what do I do next, how am I supposed to survive this?"
- "I was so mad at God—I felt like I had nothing to believe in. She didn't criticize me for that."
- "It was nice to have an objective person tell me it wasn't my fault. He seemed so sure I was going to be okay. I thought, 'He's the expert. Maybe he knows or sees something I don't!' "

Treatment failure is often caused by differing expectations between therapist and client. All goal setting should be collaborative. Some suggested treatment guidelines are as follows.

Treatment Goals

1. *Allow the client to vent.* The individual may feel a need to verbally and emotionally process the traumatic event, though emotional responses are generally constricted initially. This does not mean the client will not cry or express anger or sadness immediately following the event, but that affective acknowledgment is generally delayed by defensive reactions designed to protect the mourner. Ventilation is a normal, healthy response to a terrifying event, and the therapist can use this initial period of emotional processing to collect assessment data about the individual's level of functioning and adaptive capacities. Those around the individual may grow tired of hearing the same stories repeatedly, but the therapist should exercise patience and use these sessions to establish rapport and trust.

2. *Help the client identify symptoms of distress.* As the client processes the event, the therapist can facilitate change by empowering the client. Due to the disruption in the individual's life and the ensuing period of shock and denial, the client may need assistance in identifying symptoms of emotional distress. This process involves uncovering the feelings behind the thoughts, behaviors, or actions. Since emotional constriction

during this time can be an adaptive mechanism protecting survivors from affective responses they are not yet able to deal with, this process must be regulated in a skillful manner by the attending therapist. Validation of these reactions as normal helps to decrease the anxiety produced by the underlying powerful and overwhelming emotions.

3. *Educate.* As the client emotionally and cognitively processes and identifies the emotional impact of the trauma, the therapist can take the opportunity to educate the client about the normal and usual reactions to events similar to the one they experienced. At this time, the "stages of grief" as well as the complications of trauma can be explained to the mourner. This is also the time to dispel myths about grief (course of bereavement, time factors, etc.). This process helps clients to validate their experience as normal. Alice, a 44-year-old mother of a deceased murder victim, once stated, "If only I had known that what I was experiencing was not crazy or strange, I could have saved myself a lot of worry and shame. I was afraid to be around other people for fear they would discover how disturbed I was." Since very few traumatized mourners have experienced a traumatic loss before, it is incumbent upon the therapist to provide this frame of reference.

4. *Restore control.* Clients or patients should be seen as collaborators or partners in the therapeutic process. As the therapist educates them, the information becomes a catalyst for empowering them. By allowing the survivor-victims to become "experts" in their own recovery, the therapist is empowering them and restoring a sense of control to their life, which has been compromised by the traumatic incident. They can then use this information to educate those similarly affected, thereby shifting the focus off of themselves and on to others and encouraging social integration.

5. *Provide support.* As discussed at length, an important variable in the recovery of the individual from any type of trauma is the level of social attachment, integration, and support. Initially, the client may feel wary of trusting others and may isolate from those who normally provide healthy sources of support. The therapist may initially be the only social resource utilized by the client. The therapist should present as a calm, reassuring, and knowledgeable source of support. Once trust is established, the client should be encouraged to begin developing a supportive network. The therapist may provide referrals to healthy support groups or networks or individuals seeking similar support.

6. *Reduce self-blame.* As the individual cognitively processes the events before, during, and after the trauma, the therapist can utilize cognitive techniques to challenge irrational, self-blaming thoughts. Providing information about the traumatic grief process allows the individual to

discover that self-blame, guilt, and shame are common reactions and can be purposeful in nature. As the individual struggles with the impact of random violence and the personal vulnerability of humans, it is only natural to try to assign blame. To admit that humans are truly vulnerable creatures who cannot be shielded from random violence often causes extreme distress. Therefore, the survivor-victim may assume responsibility for the outcome, thereby promoting a cause-effect relationship that allows for individual control over the environment. Insight-oriented therapies that explain the function of these reactions can be useful in minimizing the intensity and duration of this response.

7. *Help the individual regulate physiological symptoms of arousal.* As previously discussed, a traumatic event acts as an unconditioned stimulus that elicits autonomic distress. Kardiner (1941) used the term *physioneurosis* to describe the activities of the Autonomic Nervous System (ANS). After a trauma, the ANS appears to continue to prepare the individual for arousal. Measurements of urinary norepinephrine metabolites in Vietnam veterans with post-trauma stress have shown chronic elevation in noradrenergic activity, as compared to controls with other psychiatric diagnoses (Ochberg, 1988). It seems the individual may become habituated to the original trauma stimuli, although associated events may cause the increased physiological arousal. Intrinsically nonthreatening cues associated with the trauma become the conditioned stimulus (CS). The CS is then capable of eliciting a defensive reaction (conditioned reaction) (Pavlov, 1927). The increased arousal leads to an intensification of all emotional reactions.

There seems to be a consensus in the literature (Ingram, 1986; Thompson, 1988)) that increases in adrenalin secretion during arousal may intensify anger and anxiety under stressful conditions. It may be suggested, therefore, that the intensity of the autonomic arousal in traumatized mourners causes them to go directly from stimulus to response, without making the cognitive connection between actual threat and the arousal response. Autonomic arousal no longer acts as the physiological preparation for trauma, but acts as the precipitating agent for fear and arousal.

If we apply a cognitive model of emotions, the assumption could be made that psychophysiological symptoms of arousal can be traced to an interaction of cognitive disturbance and genetically determined patterns of physiological activity. Following the tenets of cognitive theory, an individual's cognitive evaluation of the physiological response leads to psychological reactions. To this end, it would seem that therapy should assist the individual to: (a) become aware of the connection between cognitions and their emotional response; (b) promote some cognitive distancing from the physiological reaction; (c) reframe the cognitive appraisal of the event; and (d) decrease the subjective experience of anxiety and intensity of the arousal.

In Chapter 5 on page 64, the case of Margaret was presented as a means of demonstrating this type of interactive process. The central issue of treatment was to promote a sense of mastery over the situation and integrate the meaning of the traumatic experience. In Margaret's case, her cognitive interpretation of the experience led to physiological, behavioral, and affective disturbances in a nonlinear fashion.

An experiential approach to treatment was utilized, allowing Margaret to have full responsibility and choice over the entire treatment process. (Note: this approach may be contraindicated in those with confounding Axis II pathology.) During an interactive exercise of self-encountering, Margaret was encouraged to nurture and comfort her wounded self. By turning inward for nurturance and acceptance, Margaret began to reestablish an internal locus of control. After initial reports of feeling "emotionally drained," Margaret reported a sense of release from the role of being a victim. The symptoms of hyperarousal began to dissipate and subsequently her need to drink decreased, as did the other symptomatology.

Exposure therapies such as systematic desensitization following muscle relaxation training allow for coupling of the stimulus and relaxation response and may desensitize the individual to incapacitating fears and anxieties. Stress management techniques such as generalized relaxation training, biofeedback, and self-hypnosis have been used to decrease symptoms of arousal. These techniques allow for an interruption to be made in the automatic loop between stimulus and response by making possible conscious self-regulation and therefore disengaging the general anxiety reactions developed after the trauma. The individual develops a newly perceived, self-regulated contingency between stimulus and response.

Caution should be exercised with techniques such as hypnosis, which may imply a loss of control by the individual. Systematic desensitization or any other technique that includes a reliving of the trauma may not necessarily be adaptive to the individual. Cognitive and emotional replay may be followed by a conditioned endorphine release and subsequent hyperactivity. Therefore, the individual's response to all therapy should be monitored closely, and individual coping resources should be evaluated prior to any therapeutic endeavor.

8. *Promote mastery over the trauma and integrate the meaning of the traumatic experience.* It has been said that there is no "goodness of fit" between traumatized individuals and their environment. Traumatized

clients view the world as a threatening place where they are not safe. The myth of invulnerability has been shattered and the individual is left with the task of redefining "normal."

Although the underlying belief of "invulnerability" may be a cognitive distortion, experiential approaches can be an effective method of dealing with trauma mastery and redefining normal. The basic value premise in experiential psychology permits clients to have full responsibility and choice over the treatment process. The responsibility of choice empowers traumatized clients and encourages them to regain control over their lives. Experiential methods generally include an interactive stage of self-encountering that promotes self-love, self-protection, and self-nurturance. When clients are taught to turn inward for nurturance and control, they are reestablishing an internal locus of control. They no longer need to rely on cognitive distortions for self-protection, but can begin to attach new meanings to life events. In this way, they can reestablish systemic equilibrium.

9. *Focus on any inadequacies of awareness, arousal, or affective expression.* While affective, cognitive, behavioral, and physiological constriction may initially serve self-protective purposes, there comes a point in the grieving process that this repression becomes maladaptive. While there are no exact time parameters for any one phase of traumatic grief, the therapist should see evidence of change over time. This nonlinear process involves different levels of awareness, arousal, and expression. A client whose presenting symptomatology is static may develop difficulties in other levels of personality functioning (interpersonal, individual-social). Education, support, validation, insight, and experiential approaches should be pursued in a nonthreatening manner.

10. *Identify restructured roles.* Despite the role of the deceased in the survivor's life, there are significant systemic changes that require a redefinition of role assignment. Survivors may find adjustment to these changes as symbolic of their ability to successfully adapt to the loss. Systems approaches (communications systems therapy, structural therapy, Bowen family systems therapy), which maintain that individuals are best understood in the context in which they exist, are best suited for this type of task.

11. *Ask clients to describe the future.* Before clients can understand what it takes to recover from adversity, they must understand what it will be like when they achieve this task. Ask questions such as, "If you were not struggling with your grief anymore, what would you be doing? How would you be feeling? What would you be thinking about? How would you be acting?" Solution-focused methods can be useful in refocusing the therapeutic process, but should be utilized with discretion. Imple-

mentation of these methods too early in the bereavement process may discourage and minimize the normal, healthy responses that are necessary for adaptation.

12. *Help the client say good-bye.* The abruptness of a traumatic event usually prohibits the resolution of unfinished business between the survivor and the deceased. The nature of the relationship at the time of death can become a significant issue for survivors as they progress through the grief process. Gestalt methods create a situation in which clients can psychodramatically encounter the deceased. There are three important elements to the Empty Chair monologue or the Empty Chair dialogue: appreciations, resentments and regrets. Saying good-bye to the deceased usually represents a significant movement toward successful adaptation. The timing of this task is part of the artistry of successful trauma therapy. Premature initiation of this task can produce frustration in the client as well as the therapist.

General Guidelines to Follow

1. *Always request a physical examination by a medical doctor.* It is important to rule out any physical causes of psychopathology and to uncover any physical problems prior to initiating therapy. In cases where physical problems do exist, it is advisable to periodically collaborate with the primary care physician.

2. *Do not act horrified.* It is important that the therapist not act overwhelmed or horrified as the client replays the circumstances specific to the traumatic event. Clients need to know that they can discuss even the most horrible aspects of the trauma and that the therapist can handle this type of discussion. The last thing the client needs at this point is to have to protect the therapist from the tragedy. This is not to say, however, that the therapist should avoid labeling the event as "horrible" or "tragic" when appropriate and necessary for validation purposes.

3. *Provide adequate role induction.* The role-induction process is particularly important with the grieving client, as it becomes the cornerstone for developing trust. Expectations (from both sides) should be discussed thoroughly and a contract should be developed outlining what the participants can expect. The process of grief resolution is not a linear process that continually and gradually becomes easier until the client achieves total adaptation; rather, it is a circular process that produces intermittent periods of intense sadness and grief, regardless of the point achieved along the continuum. Explaining this process is part of the initial role-induction process and encourages healthy, realistic goal setting.

Maintenance and Support

The process of traumatic grief resolution is not a linear, progressive process, but rather a series of emotional challenges that may intermittently appear over time. It is not uncommon for a mourner to report a significant decrease in certain emotions such as anger, sadness, or guilt, only to find the same symptom(s) rekindled at an anniversary date, birthday, etc.

It is incumbent upon the clinician to prepare the mourner for the "waxing and waning" of symptoms that may be perceived as failure or an emotional setback. Once realistic expectations for recovery have been set, the client will experience less distress if the process of bereavement does not follow a predictable course.

The frequency and duration of any clinical intervention should be consistent with the mourner's perception of need. Scheduling weekly sessions may provide the necessary support to those who are socially isolated or withdrawn, but may not correspond to the emotional needs of the individual. Remember, the process of grief, even traumatic grief, is a reactive function. Clinical interventions may be scheduled on an as-needed basis, unless there is significant impairment in functioning that necessitates more frequent, consistent intervention.

Despite the natural, reactive qualities of traumatic grief, the supportive nature of the clinical intervention may be an essential element in the resolution process. The nature of the therapeutic relationship may serve to buffer the effects of the trauma, increase self-esteem, and alter the client's role functioning, thereby mitigating the impact of the event.

The duration of the traumatic grief disturbance is dependent upon the personal characteristics and social and environmental influences on the individual mourner. Clinicians should study, seek supervision, and be aware of transference and countertransference issues that may arise throughout the intervention.

Vicarious Traumatization

Clinicians who work with traumatized populations are exposed to repeated verbal and affective reminders of an array of atrocities experienced by their clients. Continual exposure to painful material that cannot be assimilated or processed (due to a lack of structured formats for this type of work) may result in symptoms of burnout or countertransference and threaten the mental health of the clinician, as well as interfering with the therapeutic process.

McMann and Pearlman (1990) describe the contributing factors to therapist burnout as including: "professional isolation, the emotional drain of always being empathetic, ambiguous successes, lack of therapeutic success, nonreciprocated giving and attentiveness, failure to live up to one's own expectations, leading to feelings of inadequacy or incompetence" (p. 133). Burnout generally produces symptoms such as depression, cynicism, boredom, loss of compassion, and discouragement.

Countertransference, on the other hand, refers to the unresolved conflicts or traumas in the therapist's past that are reactivated by repeated exposure to traumatic material. The symptomatology produced by the countertransference process parallels the PTSD response of the direct victim, including: intrusive imagery, rage, guilt and shame, grief and mourning, inability to concentrate, denial, numbing, and detachment.

Vicarious traumatization, then, refers to both the exposure to painful, graphic, traumatic material and the appraisal of the therapeutic process in light of the therapist's beliefs, expectations, and assumptions. During supervisory sessions with staff therapists at a mental health center that provides services to victims of crime, the following trends were detected.

1. Therapists who work solely with victims of crime risk vicarious victimization via constant exposure to intense suffering and traumatic graphic content.
2. Over time, the therapist's view of the world can become distorted, with the misperception that evil and tragedy are the rule rather than the exception.
3. The therapist's own sense of safety, control over the environment, and frame of reference may be transformed due to overexposure to the aftermath of trauma.
4. Many therapists complain that those close to them (friends and families) are often insensitive to or do not understand the seriousness of their work and the extent of devastation caused by the trauma. Some do not understand why others are not as outraged as they are.
5. The effects of the social resources utilized by therapists may be attenuated or negated if the therapist withdraws from these once positive sources of support.

McMann and Pearlman (1990) support these observations when they note that trauma disrupts the client and therapist's conceptualizations of trust, safety, power, independence, esteem, intimacy, and frame of reference. These researchers outline the following strategies for prevention of and recovery from various traumatization.

1. Maintain a healthy personal and professional balance.
2. Achieve a balance between professional responsibilities such as therapy, research, teaching, public speaking, etc.
3. Balance caseload responsibilities between victim and nonvictim cases.
4. Respect personal boundaries. Plan for time off, set a realistic work schedule limiting weekend and evening work, and make time for supervision and consultation when needed.
5. Develop realistic expectations and goals regarding clinical outcomes.
6. Accept permission to experience fully the emotions produced during the therapeutic encounter.
7. Find ways to self-nurture and self-support.
8. Engage in activities that promote social or political change.
9. Seek out nonvictim-related activities that provide hope and healthy support.

CONCLUSION

Therapeutic work with trauma victims requires a thorough understanding of the dynamics involved in the victimization process as well as of the therapeutic focus related to different levels of personality and functioning throughout the adaptation process. The therapist must consider not only the reactive, individualized nature of the response, but also the transference and countertransference issues that may arise and complicate the process of recovery.

III

STIGMATIZED GRIEF

10

A Theoretical Overview of Stigmatized Grief

Societal reaction to death shows many faces. When death follows the natural course, that is, in old age and as a consequence of the aging process, grief is sanctioned by society. Reasonably clear rituals have been established in the case of natural death to guide the behavior of the bereaved as well as that of the caregivers and observers. This is the more common experience.

Some deaths are altruistic in nature and seen as having occurred for a noble cause. To reward these types of death, some posthumous recognition may be given. For example, if the noble death occurred during wartime as a result of a heroic action by a member of the military service in combat, the symbol of recognition is the Congressional Medal of Honor. Similar recognitions are awarded in the civilian community.

At the other extreme, there are those deaths that are perceived as not being worthy of open sanction by society. These are the so-called stigmatized deaths. Foremost among them are deaths caused by AIDS and suicide. Death in both instances would be classified by Goffman (1963) as falling within the stigma category of "blemishes of individual character." In cases of stigmatized death, the grief is then disenfranchised. Society may signal that the bereaved does not have a legitimate right to grieve the loss by making the mourner feel ashamed. AIDS-related death is a relatively recent phenomenon, whereas society has struggled with the proper stance to take toward suicidal death for thousands of years. Several parallels and contrasts are apparent in both types of death.

Suicide is sudden and, therefore, usually denies opportunity for antici-

139

patory grief. It is also often violent. Post-traumatic Stress Syndrome (PTSD) may complicate the bereavement process for the person who may have witnessed the suicide or discovered the dead body. Sudden death is thought by some to be more difficult to cope with than a death that has allowed time for the survivor to prepare for it. Failure to have recognized the suicide potential of the victim may arouse severe feelings of guilt in the survivor. The most affected persons are invariably those who have had a significant relationship with the victim.

AIDS-related death, in contrast, follows a progressive course, although the pace of the progression is highly individualized. During the HIV-positive period, observable physical changes are generally absent, and from outward appearances life continues as usual. Hope is high so denial may interfere with family and friends' ability to realistically evaluate their loved one's future. Therefore, anticipatory grief work is problematic. This stance is reinforced since the person may have minimal, if any, limitations placed upon previous daily functioning. When full-blown AIDS is evident, the downhill course may be rapid. Similar to suicide, survivors are likely to have had significant relationships with the deceased. Ambivalence may be present in either situation, which furthers the probability of complicated bereavement. In both instances, AIDS and suicide, the bereaved are subjected to courtesy stigma (Goffman, 1963), which may be acquired by simple association with the victim. Caregivers of persons who die of AIDS are often suspected to be homosexual themselves. Courtesy stigma is therefore accorded to them.

The fear of contagion is present in both. With suicide, there is concern about familial inheritability. A fairly common belief is that if one person in a family commits suicide other members are likely to see this as a way of solving problems. With AIDS, there is concern by caregivers about physical contagion, as well as about the condemnatory attitudes of society. Stigma pervades both situations and is likely to lead to social isolation. Lack of social support has a negative impact upon recovery from bereavement.

Blame is placed upon the victim in both instances. AIDS victims are looked upon pejoratively because of their assumed life style. Suicide victims are viewed negatively because of a supposed character weakness that led them to look for an "easy" way out of their difficulty rather than utilizing more mature coping strategies. Taking one's own life is not acceptable. Even if the suicide is explained on the basis of mental illness, being crazy is similarly stigmatizing. A diagnosis of mental illness means the individual was not "strong" enough to deal with life's demands. Being weak is unforgivable.

Where suicide is involved, society also castigates the survivor for not having taken some action that would have prevented the suicide. In other words, the significant other should have been sensitive and insightful enough to recognize that the victim was suicidal. As for AIDS victims, they should not have transgressed against the teachings of the Bible and engaged in same-gender sex or other behavior viewed as inappropriate or high risk by society. Therefore, they deserve the abomination that has befallen them. These attitudes are even directed at those who acquire the HIV virus via blood transfusions or needle pricks.

For these reason, and more, the grief for AIDS and suicide victims is disenfranchised. Survivors are denied the usual means of bereavement. Prominent among these deprivations is the loss of social support, forcing the survivors to grieve in silence and alone. The literature is replete with examples and admonitions that reflect the confusion of society regarding the appropriate way to relate to the survivor. Avoidance and/or a conspiracy of silence evolve. A situation has thus been created that is fraught with the potential for complicated grief. It is generally accepted that bereaved persons need to have the opportunity to share their feelings, thoughts, and moods with others. When open communication is missing, the disenfranchised must carry an additional burden at the very time that he or she is least able to do so.

Doka (1989) clarifies the concept of disenfranchisement further. For something to be disenfranchised, the right or privilege must have been possessed in the first place. From earliest prehistoric times, communities or societies have developed a system of privileges or rights for all of its members. These enfranchised rights could be shared and expressed openly. Over the centuries, ideas relative to enfranchisement have changed and as a result certain rights and privileges have been disenfranchised. Among these have been ideas regarding grief.

According to Doka (1989) there are three general types of disenfranchised grief. The first type includes those individuals "whose relationships are socially unrecognized, illegitimate, or in other ways unsanctioned" (p. 14). This would encompass homosexual relationships. A second type includes those persons whose loss does not fit the typical norms of appropriateness. Perhaps here one could include individuals grieving the loss of a loved one who committed suicide. Doka's third type includes those people whose ability to grieve is in question or who are thought not to be legitimate grievers. Conceivably, here one could think of an unrecognized partner or other significant others not legally recognized. In spite of these beliefs and attitudes, all of these individuals undoubtedly grieve in their own way. Problems commence when the grief is disenfranchised.

Doka (1989), the major proponent of the disenfranchised grief construct, invited several writers to discuss relationships, losses, and grievers. These three aspects will be discussed briefly, beginning with disenfranchised relationships. Presented in this category are several situations that do not typically come to mind when one thinks of grieving. Among these are relationships involving lovers, foster parents, extramarital affairs, and ex-spouses.

Fuller, Geis, and Rush (1988) focus upon homosexual love relationships. Less attention was paid to this type of relationship prior to the AIDS outbreak. As AIDS emerged as a major public health problem, all of the stereotypes of gross promiscuity and a "bathhouse" subculture incited increased negativism and hostility toward homosexual relationships. If the deceased was homosexual, caregivers and grievers may be assumed likewise to be gay. Homophobia intensified, moving gay relationships into a minority group category that aroused fear and hate. Disenfranchisement of the relationship and of grief, if AIDS appeared, was a consequence that was almost expected.

Occasional media attention addresses the issue of foster-parent relationships when an attempt is made to legally adopt the foster child and opposition is presented by forces such as child protective agencies or natural parents. The vehemence, tenacity, and emotional and financial sacrifice attest to the trauma wrought upon the protagonists when the relationship is threatened by potential disruption. Depending upon the side of the fence one is on, the relationship may be seen as legitimate or disenfranchised. One can only guess at the innumerable times this situation occurs but passes unnoticed without social attention.

Many dyadic relationships are of sufficient intensity that they engage a significant part of the life of the involved individuals. Yet these relationships may well be disenfranchised. In addition to the aforementioned homosexual bonds, society does not condone extramarital affairs. A variable that also affects this type of relationship is the openness or secrecy of the affair. The usual sources of social support are not available and, if death occurs, mourning rituals are usually not available. If the relationship has been secret, the bereaved may have no one to turn to for solace.

Folta and Deck (1989) address the issue of disenfranchisement and friends. In spite of the fact that friendship relationships are important, and especially so due to urbanization and mobility, which decrease the opportunity for kinship involvement, friendships are ignored or overlooked. As the population ages, there is increased likelihood of the elderly depending primarily on friendships for social networks because of their propinquity or simply because the older person has outlived nuclear and extended family. Younger persons also, for a myriad of reasons, may have developed relationships that outweigh the importance at that time of kinship ties. Cultural, societal, and legal factors place the familial ties as paramount. Friendships take a subordinate role and often are denied even the notification of death if the biological family is not accepting of the friend.

Ex-spouses also are faced with special relationship problems due to the disenfranchisement. Unique problems are posed because of the ambiguous nature of the relationship. Some type of continuing contact may be inherent because of children, former in-laws, or other factors. Readjustment of the old relationship with the ex-spouse is necessary and a new one must be established, whether friendly or antagonistic. If illness or death occurs, the ex-spouse is an outsider. No protocols are in place to guide social intercourse relative to visiting during the period of illness, nor to the proper stance to take in the case of death. This may be even more pronounced if the ex-spouse has remarried. For example, if there are children, they may be welcomed at the funeral and seated with family. Unclear is the seating arrangement and role of the ex-spouse; in fact, even attendance at the funeral may be questioned. The word "ex" is itself instructive because it connotes the cessation of the existence of an entity that previously existed. An ex-spouse can truly be between the proverbial rock and a hard place in view of the disenfranchisement of the relationship.

Several losses are considered not to be important enough to grieve about. Among these are perinatal losses, which are disenfranchised because supposedly there has not been time for bonding to develop (see Chapter 3). Society, similarly, tends to look askance at individuals who seem to grieve too deeply over loss due to a miscarriage. Until "right to life" proponents seized upon abortion as an action that may have long-term grief consequences, this was not seen as an occurrence warranting bereavement behaviors. Perhaps a majority of people still discount abortion as being worthy of intense grief. Household pet loss is accepted as warranting some level of grief, but for the most part it is disenfranchised. Pet morticians, however, recognized years ago that pet loss mourning rituals offered a profitable business opportunity and proceeded to capitalize upon it.

It is clearly evident that a myriad of losses and relationships are not sanctioned by society and as a result they are stigmatized and/or disenfranchised. Grievers are therefore categorized relative to a hypothetical continuum ranging from legitimacy to stigmatized to disenfranchisement.

There is a real need to examine thoroughly the effect of stigma and disenfranchisement upon the grief process. Likewise, it is important to explore how survivors deal with the multiple other variables that affect grief. This section, although limited to bereavement following death from AIDS and from suicide, is intended to be a step in this direction.

11

The Process of Grief After an
AIDS-Related Death

AIDS is a viral syndrome that strips the body's immune system of its ability to defend itself against life-threatening illness. The Centers for Disease Control and Prevention (1994) reports 243,423 AIDS-related deaths as of June 1994. Upon their death, the victims of AIDS leave behind a bereaved population of family and friends whose grief process is complicated by the mode of death in a unique manner.

Public attitudes toward people with AIDS (PWA) and their mourners are influenced by a complex set of factors that are tied to the characteristics of the disease. Not only is AIDS a lethal, transmittable disease, it carries with it a stigma indicative of a social judgment process regarding the nature and cause of the illness and subsequent death. The stigma attached to this form of death stems from a number of factors: (a) the physical destruction of the body throughout the course of the illness (lesions, severe weight loss, etc.); (b) its perceived communicability (often based on myths and misinformation); (c) the inevitable lethality of the disease; and (d) its prevalence among already stigmatized groups (i.e., homosexuals, IV drug users, or minorities).

The terms *discredited* versus *discreditable* (first coined by Goffman in 1963) are used to differentiate specific attributes possessed by stigmatized individuals. Discredited individuals are stigmatized due to undesirable characteristics, such as physical deformities and mental illness, that are considered by society as discrediting in any situation. The discreditable individuals (i.e., the PWA) possess an attribute that would be stigmatizing if discovered. The discrediting characteristic (having AIDS), coupled with a societal bias against, for example, the life style, behavior,

145

or socioeconomic status of the individual, creates a stigma that others treat as all-important in defining the person.

Unfortunately, this stigma is often generalized to the family and friends of the PWA and is referred to conceptually as "courtesy" stigma (Goffman, 1963).

Prejudicial attitudes of the perceiver, social cues, and the social cognitive processes involved in interpreting these cues seem to be key variables in determining the occurrence of courtesy stigmatization.

The tenets of attribution theory provide a framework for understanding these social judgment processes and their impact on PWA and the bereaved. Attributions of responsibility for acquiring AIDS implies a social judgment or evaluation of another person's behavior to determine the extent to which their behavior was a factor in the acquisition of the disease. This evaluation centers around four dimensions: (a) the extent to which the behavior caused the situation; (b) the extent to which the person knew or should have known the potential consequences of the behavior; (c) the extent to which the person intended to engage in the behavior; and (d) the extent to which factors over which the person had little or no control might have influenced the behavior (Shaver, 1985).

This process of attribution has an impact on the social resources available for the PWA and the bereaved by influencing the availability of help-giving resources. Clinicians or other caregivers who concern themselves with who deserves attention or help and who does not, based upon their perception of the individual's responsibility for having the disease, create and exacerbate a "social death" climate for the individual that can be as traumatic as the physical death.

Many researchers have also found evidence of the social judgment process in their study of the AIDS epidemic. Herek and Glunt (1991), in their study of AIDS-related attitudes, found that 51.6% of their sample ($n = 925$) believed that PWA were a serious risk to the rest of society. Since the average person who contracts AIDS may be asymptomatic for up to 10 years after initial infection, this perceived risk may be generalized to those close to the deceased, causing the usual social resources to withdraw and/or be unavailable for fear of "catching the disease" from the bereaved who may not know as yet that they, too, are infected. Because AIDS is such a devastating disease with no known cure at this time, the threat of acquiring the disease causes significant distress and often a need to place blame.

The majority of information on the grief process following an AIDS-related death focuses on the grief-related symptoms of gay men. There is a paucity of literature addressing AIDS-related bereavement for survivors of IV drug users, hemophiliacs, bisexuals, racial minorities, women, infants and children, AIDS suicides, and needle-prick cases, as well as others.

Clearly, AIDS is not a gay disease. Goodgame (1990), Novello (1991), and Brookmeyer (1991) document heterosexual transmission via sexual intercourse as the primary route of HIV infection, accounting for 75% of the cases worldwide. The Centers for Disease Control and Prevention (1994) report 27,281 cases of AIDS via heterosexual transmission by mid-1994. Despite public disclosure by self-reported heterosexual, non-drug-using celebrities such as Magic Johnson and Arthur Ashe that they, too, had been infected by the AIDS virus, the gay stigma remains.

Understanding how these attitudes impact the process of bereavement for the surviving family and friends of AIDS victims requires sorting through the circumstances, dynamics, and relationships involved in many different situations. The following discussions will examine the factors impacting the bereavement process and describe a typology of symptomatology inherent to this type of grief. Knowledge of these issues is essential to the development of intervention strategies and research studies pertinent to AIDS-related bereavement.

FACTORS IMPACTING THE GRIEF PROCESS

As with traumatic grief, stigmatized grief is complicated by the mode of death and the manner in which the event is interpreted and integrated within the mourner's frame of reference. A personal construct psychology model of bereavement can be used to explain this process. Constructs allow individuals to interpret their environments and develop meaning from their experiences. Normal manifestations of the grief process, such as shock, denial, and anger, challenge the individual's construct system and eventually lead to construct system dislocation (a maladaptive assimilation of events) or adaptation.

The death of a loved one to AIDS may mean the loss of the person who confirmed the mourner's view of the world. Separation from others (due to social withdrawal or stigma), threat of contracting the disease, and other factors impede the mourner's assimilation of the event in an adaptive manner. To adequately assess the mourner's psychosocial functioning following an AIDS-related death, some of these factors impacting the bereavement process should be explored further. In addition to the clinical experience and case examples provided by the authors, the empirical work of Bergeron and Handley (1992), Trice (1988), Weinbach (1989), Viney, Henry, Walker, and Crooks (1992), Geis and Fuller (1986), Riley and Green (1993), and Martin (1988) will be presented.

Appraised Vulnerability to AIDS

Spouses or significant others who lose a loved one to AIDS must face the possibility that they, too, may have been infected with the HIV virus and they fear the pain and suffering they have witnessed in their loved one. AIDS is mentally and physically destructive to the human body. Not only will the PWA often develop lesions and experience severe weight loss and other forms of physical deterioration, mental transformations may also occur.

AIDS encephalopathy (also known as AIDS dementia) is the most common neurologic manifestation of AIDS. In the early stages it is often misdiagnosed as depression, as the initial signs and symptoms manifest as social withdrawal, apathy, psychiatric retardation, and deficits in concentration and/or memory. The prognosis of AIDS dementia is poor and the symptomatology presented increases to include motor deficits, seizures, decreased levels of consciousness, aphasia, and apraxia. The mourners of PWA who develop the AIDS dementia complex witness a complete transformation of their loved one, both mentally and physically, in a traumatic and humiliating manner. The impact of witnessing such a deterioration of the body and mind is especially alarming if the fear of acquiring the same symptomatology is a legitimate concern.

Geis and Fuller (1986) outlined three types of responses to the question, "How do you feel about your own exposure to AIDS?" These attitudes include: (a) fatalism ("If it is my time to go, I'll go"); (b) obsession ("I think about it all the time"); and (c) rationalization, attempting to find peace or security by making or accepting sometimes irrational arguments for or against the probability of acquiring the disease. It is not uncommon for a clinician to encounter a grieving client who experiences all these reactions simultaneously, or clients who are constantly reassessing their own vulnerability toward the disease.

For those who have already tested HIV positive, not only must they deal with the death of their loved one, they may be struggling with the fear of their own death and dying. This struggle may produce existential anxiety and intrapersonal crisis. Those perceived by friends, family, and society as "infected" must face the social stigma of the illness as well as the social isolation imposed by those who fear close contact.

Lack of Traditional Recognition

If the relationship was a nontraditional one, the bereaved may not receive the usual recognition given to a spouse by family, friends, or coworkers due to a failure of society to recognize the nature of the relationship. Clandestine relationships of this type may not be condoned by the family, friends, or society because they may not be perceived as socially, politically, religiously, or legally sanctioned. Weinbach (1989) writes, "Kinship seems to be the principal criterion for legitimacy of grief and mourning in our society, and, to a lesser degree within the helping profession" (p. 57). These mourners may not be included in many of the traditional rituals and customs associated with the mourning process due to the nature of their relationship with the deceased. Some examples include:

1. *Being denied access to the dying individual in the hospital.* Most hospital ICU/CCU departments allow only recognized family members visitation. Denial of access may prevent the mourner from saying goodbye to the deceased or achieving closure.
2. *Lack of death notification.* Death notification is generally provided to the "next of kin," usually a blood relative of the deceased or a spouse, leaving the unrecognized mourner to discover the death by chance.
3. *Lack of mourning aids.* Sympathy cards, participation in funeral planning, and participation in the funeral service usually include recognized relatives of the deceased. Partners in nontraditional relationships may be excluded from these events and/or may not receive this type of recognition.
4. *Legal unpreparedness.* Most individuals find confronting their own mortality a difficult task; therefore, wills are not common, especially among the young. Homosexual relationships are not legally sanctioned via a marital contract and thus receive no legal recognition following the death of one of the partners. Without a will or specific instructions regarding the distribution of belongings, partners in homosexual relationships have limited access to tangible items belonging to the deceased that may have sentimental or monetary value. Efforts to retrieve these items may lead to conflict with the partner's family.
5. *Loss of social support.* Not only is the deceased excluded from some of the rituals and customs associated with the process of death and dying, many of the social support systems utilized by other mourners may be unavailable, limited, or destroyed. In a homosexual community, for example, the deceased may have witnessed the decimation of their entire social network, due to multiple deaths. If the loss occurs outside the traditional family structure, existing family networks may not be available, utilized, or helpful.

If the relationship was not legally and/or socially sanctioned, mental health resources (public or private), as well as public assistance programs, may not be available, utilized, or helpful. The survivor may be unwilling to share his/her feelings about the loss with others for fear of condemnation and social disapproval.

Condemnation

Family members or friends of the deceased who choose to discuss their loss with others may be the recipients of responses such as, "If they hadn't . . . (been that way, behaved in that way, or made such poor decisions) . . . they wouldn't have died," "It was their fault," "You should have . . . ," "This is God's way of punishing them," etc. These types of response serve to minimize, delegitimize, and diminish the loss for the survivors.

Fuller and Geis (1985) outline precursors to acceptance of the survivor's grief by the dominant society. These authors found the dominant society is more likely to extend permission to grieve to nontraditional partners if the relationship has: (a) demonstrated devotion, but not blatant sexuality; (b) fulfilled the expectations of the biological families; (c) received familial support as exemplified by an engagement; and (d) ended with an illness or accident viewed as an unfortunate occurrence. As discussed earlier, attitudes toward PWA and AIDS-related deaths are quite diverse and complex. Permission to grieve may become dependent upon the mourner's fulfillment of social expectations that are ambiguous, inconsistent, and tied to the emotional needs of the dominant society rather than to their own.

Some mourners may internalize the shame and stigma surrounding the death, leading to self-denigration, ignominy, disgrace, and a feeling of rejection, which may in turn lead to subsequent inter- and intrapersonal conflict. Mahoney (1991) speaks to this phenomenon when he writes, "Rejection is not confined to interpersonal relationships: neglect, rejection, and abuse can be intrapersonal. It is, indeed, when these patterns become internalized and identified with that they become most powerful and tenacious in their influence on a life" (p. 343).

Religion

When a loved one dies of AIDS, religious beliefs can help or hinder grief work as the individual attempts to deal with the death. A major loss often promotes a quest for meaning, not only for the loss itself, but for the mourner's existential understanding of life and death. Attachment theory suggests that throughout the process of evolution, instinctual development centered around the belief that losses were retrievable, as witnessed in the instinctual response of animals. Behavioral grief responses in animals are geared toward reestablishing a relationship with the lost attachment figure (Bowlby, 1973). A similar response in humans is exhibited in the universal attempt to regain the lost loved object through a belief in an afterlife where one can rejoin the loved one. Religion and/or spiritualism can become a source of comforting support, strength, and hope by providing an established framework in which the mourner can define and adapt to the loss.

But do the positive influences of religion and/or spiritualism hold true for the bereaved following an AIDS-related death? Previous research on religion and grief (Bowlby, 1973; Parkes & Weiss, 1983; Stephens, 1972) seems not to be generalizable to AIDS-related grief, as the respondents in these studies suffered from nonstigmatized bereavement. In fact, empirical evidence outlining the role of religion in the AIDS-related bereavement process is scarce at best. Anecdotal evidence suggests that religion can become the most devastating tool by which PWA and their mourners are stigmatized.

The tenets of Judeo-Christian tradition show evidence of death, eternal damnation, and other forms of punishment for sexual misbehavior. Since the most common form of transmission of the disease is via sexual contact, this belief may leave the mourner, as well as the PWA, feeling guilty, ashamed, and alone. Sarah, a 28-year-old PWA, reports, "When I was in despair I turned to my church for help. The pastor told me I had been struck down by God as punishment for my sinful ways. This made me feel dirty, evil, and unworthy of forgiveness." In this situation, the social resources normally provided by religion and/or spirituality may be negated or attenuated.

Multiple Deaths

If the mourner is part of a social or family system in which multiple persons are infected with the HIV infection, bereavement overload may become a complicating factor in the process of grief by exacerbating symptomatology and causing caregiver fatigue. The mourner may be aware of the need to grieve, yet has no control over the timing of subsequent deaths. There is clinical and empirical evidence (Martin, 1988) that multiple bereavement episodes can lead to the development of Post-traumatic Stress Disorder (PTSD), Major Depressive Disorder, or other severe symptomatology, thereby complicating the process of recovery.

Ambivalent Attitudes

Interpersonal conflict over the life style of the deceased, or the actions of the deceased that led to acquisition of the disease, may lead to ambivalent feelings about the death for the survivors. The bereavement process is then complicated by anger toward the deceased (and subsequent guilt) and/or misgivings about prior interpersonal interactions. If the mourner's relationship with the deceased was a conflictual one or if multiple significant others have died, there may be prior losses (death of others, death of the relationship, etc.), which may impede the resolution of grief.

Due to the conflictual and often estranged relationships associated with some of the groups plagued with AIDS, family and friends may be unaware or uninformed about the nature and course of the illness. In many of these cases, death comes without warning, preventing good-byes and opportunities to clear up "unfinished business." Since AIDS is no respecter of age, many parents find themselves burying their children, disrupting the natural order of the life-to-death process. Parents are usually expected to precede their children in death. The untimeliness of the death can increase the sense of trauma associated with the loss.

Grief Preparation

Unlike a traumatic death, AIDS-related deaths usually provide a pre-death grief process for the mourners. Grief theorists such as Lindemann (1944) and Kübler-Ross (1969) hypothesize that the anticipatory grief process has psychological benefit for the mourners after a terminal illness (such as AIDS). The term *anticipatory grief* was first coined by Lindemann in 1944 to refer to the absence of overt manifestations of grief in survivors who had previously experienced the phases of grief and had accomplished some of the tasks of mourning prior to the actual death.

The research on the benefits of anticipatory grief is equivocal at best. Parkes (1975) found higher levels of functioning in mourners who had some advance warning of a pending death, when assessed at 13 months, than in those who had no warning. As this book points out, however, there are multiple determinants for the process of grief and mourning, including the mode of death. Forewarning of impending death is but one of the variables to be considered. Since AIDS is a protracted illness with no known cure, it can be assumed that the opportunity for some adaptation to the eventual loss may occur prior to the loss. But does this anticipatory grief process really help post-death bereavement after an AIDS-related death?

One researcher examined this question in a 1988 study of 43 mothers following the death of their sons to AIDS (Trice, 1988). The participants in this study were divided into two groups based on their status as caregivers during their son's illness and subsequent death. While all mothers in the caregiving group indicated that the care experience was personally beneficial to them and they would repeat the experience again if necessary, there is evidence that this experience had a negative effect on their psychological well-being 24–37 months following the deaths. A comparison of reported symptomatology for caregivers versus non-caregivers reveals increases in interpersonal conflict (divorce, separation), night terror, uncharacteristic violence, psychosomatic complaints, anger and rage, and job turnover in the caregiving group.

As mentioned earlier, anticipatory grief requires notification and awareness of the nature and course of the illness. Several of the mothers in the noncaregiving group indicated they were not informed of their son's illness until very near the end of the course of the disease. Due to the stigma associated with this type of death, it is possible that the benefits of the anticipatory grief process may be attenuated.

MODEL OF GRIEF

Defining the symptomatology associated with an AIDS-related death necessitates consideration of the above-mentioned variables and their impact on the process of bereavement. Although limited, there is clinical and empirical literature available that is useful in the development of this typology of grief.

The following case example illustrates the components and process of AIDS-related bereavement.

> Randy, a 34-year-old college graduate, lived with his childhood friend and fraternity brother, John, in a metropolitan area. Shortly after graduating college, Randy moved in with John, who had recently been divorced. John later revealed he was HIV positive, a condition that resulted from a blood transfusion following a motorcycle accident three years before. Randy presented for therapy 16 months after John's death from an AIDS-related condition (ARC).
>
> Randy was quick to point out that he and John were both heterosexual and questioned his therapist about her attitudes toward PWA. Randy stated he had felt forced to explain his sexual orientation to his family and friends and felt somewhat

ostracized by coworkers and acquaintances who he felt judged him unfairly because of the nature of John's death. He reported some guilt over feeling ashamed of his friend's death and even anger toward John for dying in such a dreadful manner. Throughout therapy Randy expressed anxiety over the physical deterioration of John's body near the end of his illness (lesions, severe weight loss). He felt embarrassed for John and guilt over his own discomfort.

Most prominent were issues surrounding Randy's struggle to come to terms with the injustice of his friend's death and his anger toward God for not protecting his good friend. Many times Randy asked the question, "What is the point of trying to live a decent life when there is no protection from tragedy?"

In the above example, Randy exhibits symptoms of cognitive anxiety as he tries to make sense of his experiences. The loss of bodily integrity imposed by the disease also produced anxiety for Randy as he struggled with conflicting emotions toward John (i.e., concern versus embarrassment, love versus anger and guilt, devotion versus horror). The social stigma previously referred to as "courtesy stigma" is also evident, although the circumstances surrounding John's contracting the disease were not particularly stigmatizing. Over the course of Randy's struggle with his grief, he felt increased despair as he began to view himself as different or estranged from others, who he felt did not understand his struggles. This left him feeling sad and alone.

The helplessness, loneliness, and depression associated with an AIDS-related death is of particular concern due to the increased lethality in the AIDS-bereaved population. It is proposed that the increased incidence of attempted and completed suicide found in this population is related to the anxiety and fear of death, bodily mutilation, separation and fear of loneliness, isolation, ignominy, and rejection. It seems the experience of grief is complicated by the experience of death. Increased lethality (indicative of high levels of psychological distress) then becomes a manifestation tied directly to the nature and frequency of the loss(es).

Martin (1988) surveyed a sample of 745 gay men to determine the correlations between AIDS-related bereavement and psychological distress. This study uncovered a direct dose-response relationship between bereavement episodes and the experience of: (a) traumatic stress symptomatology—ruminations, avoidance behaviors, intrusive thoughts, nightmares, panic attacks, numbing, and detachment; (b) demoralization symptoms—anxiety, dread, sadness, helplessness, hopelessness, poor self-esteem, and confusion; (c) sleep disturbance; (d) increased physician visits due to fear, and increased sense of vulnerability to AIDS and psychosomatic complaints; (e) increased use of recreational drugs (amphetamines, barbiturates, cocaine, hallucinogens); and (f) increased use of prescription drugs (benzodiazepams). The correlation between increased substance abuse and bereavement is consistent with other reports from investigators (Osterweis et al., 1984; Parkes & Brown, 1972). Since the research demonstrates that factors predictive of bereavement are also predictive of compromised health (Stroebe & Stroebe, 1987; Thompson, Breckenridge, Gallagher, & Peterson, 1984), these findings are certainly not surprising, though straightforward predictions should be made with caution.

Anger is a prevalent reaction before and after the loss. After an AIDS-related death, the survivors may experience anger in different forms: (a) anger toward the self for not protecting the deceased or for not preventing the tragedy (especially in parents); (b) anger at God for allowing the tragedy to occur (e.g., allowing the deceased to have a medical condition necessitating the need for an eventually fatal blood transfusion); (c) anger at the deceased for acting, behaving, or making decisions in a manner that caused their death; and/or (d) anger at the medical community and the health-care system, which may be perceived as insensitive and/or ineffective.

Geis and Fuller (1986) found evidence of anger toward the health community (consistent with Trice, 1988) in their study of psychosocial stress and AIDS-related bereavement. There was anger toward the medical community reported by their respondents over issues such as lack of privacy for the PWA and the family, diagnostic procedures that were invasive and unexplained, insensitivity to feelings, difficulty in diagnosis, and seemingly endless changes in treatment protocols. When they tapped the respondents' perceptions of care by various health-care professionals, it was found that nurses were reported to be more sensitive to feelings than doctors, and clinicians were usually perceived as more sensitive than researchers (because researchers cannot guarantee privacy and many patients felt like guinea pigs in the research process). One nurse reports,

> No one enjoyed working with the AIDS patients. There is so much we do not know. I was always somewhat fearful when I interacted with those patients; it was not that I was unsympathetic, I just wanted to stay healthy.

Another nurse states:

> PWAs are so needy. They seem to want your approval or validation that they are valuable human beings. Others are so angry. I can understand that, but the whole ordeal is very draining emotionally.

Anger is a natural part of grieving for both the patient and the survivor, yet (like other grief symptoms) they can impede grief resolution when prolonged or misdirected. Displaced anger, blaming, and retroflected anger (anger turned inward) all can represent serious complications to the bereavement process if prolonged. Assessment of lethality should be performed in those exhibiting evidence of retroflected anger, a reaction often overlooked because it presents very much as sadness, depression, or anxiety. Although no exact parameters for anger resolution exist, the clinician should see a balancing of feelings over time and witness some change in affective presentation by the mourner. See Table 11.1.

CONCLUSION

Families, friends, and loved ones of a PWA undergo a process of bereavement that is tied to social, political, and religious interpretations

TABLE 11.1
Multidimensional Symptom Formulation for AIDS-Related Bereavement

Affective	*Cognitive*	*Behavioral*	*Physiological*
Anger/rage/ hostility	Cognitive anxiety over loss of bodily integrity of the deceased	Interpersonal conflict: divorce, separation, job turnover	Psychosomatic complaints (migraines, hypertension)
Fear			
Depression			Sleep disturbances
Helplessness	Existential anxiety over own death and making sense of their experiences	Night terrors, nightmares	Compromised health
Hopelessness			
Numbing		Uncharacteristic violence	
Dread			
Sadness		Social isolation	
Guilt	Separation anxiety	Avoidance behaviors	
	Shame	Suicide	
	Sense of incompetence	Panic attacks	
	Self-denigration	Substance abuse	
	Ruminations	Increased visits to a physician	
	Intrusive thoughts		
	Confusion		

of life and death. The stigma associated with the manner of dying has a direct impact on the manner in which the mourners grieve the loss. AIDS produces a group of disenfranchised or secret survivors who feel shame, guilt, isolation, rejection, and self-denigration associated with the loss. Although the grief symptomatology produced by this type of death shares common characteristics with other models of grief (e.g., traumatic grief), the reasons for these manifestations are quite different. Clinicians and researchers must be acutely aware of the distinguishing characteristics of each model and the attributing factors in each. Treatment implications for AIDS-related bereavement are presented in Chapter 13.

12

The Grief Response Following Suicide

Suicide in America is a common occurrence; in fact, it is listed as the eighth leading cause of death. Conservative epidemiological figures estimate that approximately 30,000 persons commit suicide annually. McIntosh (1991) has calculated that the annual rate is 12.8 per 100,000, which means that there are 85 suicides per day or, stated in another way, one every 17 minutes. The actual number is probably much greater because of a number factors, including concealment by significant others, intentional misclassification, and variability in classificatory methods (McIntosh, 1991). More than a quarter of these suicides are committed by persons 24 years of age or younger (Ness & Pfeffer, 1990). As a result, large numbers of individuals are affected by and grieve the event. McIntosh (1991) estimates this figure to be in excess of 3,000,000. In addition, there are many more attempted suicides than completed suicides.

Considering the total number of completions, attempters, and grieving survivors, suicide can be thought of as a major public health problem. The impact is accentuated when the stigmatizing attitudes toward suicide are recognized. Suicide, by its very nature, impacts the grief process in a particularized manner, and it has generally denied the opportunity to grieve openly and have the exhibition of grief accepted by society. Suicide has an extremely inhibiting impact upon the manner in which the bereaved can express grief.

This chapter will delineate how society has viewed suicide over many centuries and how these varying perceptions have influenced the behavior of suicide survivors during the grief process. Additionally, suicide and societal response will be examined across the life span (i.e., childhood, adolescence, adulthood, and among the elderly).

CHANGING ATTITUDES TOWARD SUICIDE

The word suicide appeared in the English language in 1651. It's derivation was from the Latin term *suicidium*; *sui* is a pronoun meaning himself or herself, and *cedare* is a verb meaning to give up (Stillion, McDowell, & May, 1989). Attitudes toward suicide, however, did not wait for the term to be coined. Every society or culture has developed a perspective regarding suicide. These views have varied from acceptance to acquiescence to punitive prohibition. Over the centuries, attitudes have changed within a given culture or society. These positions have been motivated by different beliefs, religious and secular, with the latter including an economic motive. A brief longitudinal summary follows, with a focus on Western civilization.

Ancient Greece

In Greece, the birthplace of much of Western civilization, suicide was considered generally as a respectable option (Colt, 1991). Undoubtedly, the most famous of Greek suicides was that of Socrates in 399 B.C. Socrates refused an order from the State to moderate his teachings and thereby received a death penalty, which he chose to implement by drinking hemlock. This suicide is dramatically illustrated in the Jacques Louis David painting, *The Death of Socrates*. Aristotle, who had been taught by Plato, took the position that suicide was unlawful because it injures the community (Stillion et al., 1989). An example given to explicate this was that if a servant or slave committed suicide, the master was deprived of his services. Plato allowed, however, that suicide in some instances was justifiable—extraordinary sorrow, unavoidable misfortune, intolerable disgrace, or compulsion by the State. Among the ancient Greeks, suicide was therefore both condoned and abhorred, depending upon the time in history. Colt (1991) has concluded that the Greeks rationalized suicide whereas the Romans made it a sport.

Ancient Rome

Similar to the Greeks, the Romans had a goodly share of suicides that were prompted from the same motivations, to avoid disgrace and dishonor. The principle of rationality continued to guide suicidal behavior and subsequent grief. Nowhere was this more forcefully expressed than in the philosophy of the Stoics (Stillion et al., 1989), who believed in the right of an individual to kill himself if he so desired. Suicide was a noble act if performed on the basis of rationality.

Economics provided the legal basis in Roman law for forbidding suicide; singled out for this restriction were criminals, soldiers, and slaves. Numerous infractions of the law were considered felonies and therefore punishable by death and the confiscation of property. Suicide before trial saved the property of the felon for his family. Since there remained no one to bring to trial, confiscation of property did not occur. This loophole was eventually closed, with the rationale being that the act of suicide in and of itself was reason to establish guilt. The State would not be denied its reward.

As for slaves, these were the property of their master and therefore had no right to dispose of themselves—the master's property. A soldier who committed suicide had deserted his post, which was a military crime. Colt (1991), continuing his exploration of Roman thinking regarding suicide, reminds us that the mentality toward death was perhaps epitomized in the fact that "30,000 people a month were sacrificed for sport in the arenas and pet fish were fed the blood or slaves" (p. 152). During this period of Roman ascendancy, Christianity became a prominent movement, highlighted by the birth of Christ.

Christianity and Suicide

Six suicides are recorded in the Old Testament, the best known being those of Samson and King Saul. Samson's suicide was, in part, an attempt to atone for having violated his faith, whereas King Saul suicided in reaction to having suffered a significant loss, that of his three sons, in the same battle in which he himself was only wounded. All six suicides are simply recorded with no indication of moral judgment. In the New Testament, the suicide of Judas Iscariot has received the greatest attention. Again, the suicide of Judas is recorded without judgmental comment.

As time went on, attitudes toward suicide did not remain neutral, but instead an unmistakable position was taken that suicide was a sin. The godly had a responsibility to dissuade individuals from self-murder; if it should occur, the corpse and often the family survivors should be dealt with severely and in a degrading manner.

Colt (1991) has catalogued some of the methods of retribution: the corpse dragged through the streets, corpse hanged head down, property confiscated, corpse decapitated, buried outside the city, hand cut off and buried separately, hastily removed and dumped outside tribal territories, stake driven through the heart, buried under a mountain. Over the centuries, some of the more gruesome penalties were no longer exacted. However, suicide was still thought to be a mortal sin; therefore, funeral rites and/or burial in a hallowed place could be denied. Completed suicides or attempters warranted excommunication. A more enlightened society, especially during the past several centuries, considered insanity as a mitigating factor, allowing removal of sanctions from persons who had committed suicide. However charitable this action may have been intended, it introduced another stigma, that of mental illness.

There is a fertile history that has persisted over the millennia that has produced the stigmatizing perception of suicide. Although the harshness of the stigma has been softened somewhat, family members of the suicide victim endure disenfranchised grief. The concepts of disenfranchised grief and stigma will be discussed next.

DISENFRANCHISED GRIEF AND STIGMA

As indicated above, suicide has been stigmatized by society across the centuries. This stigma was not only reserved for the individual who committed suicide, but was also inflicted upon his/her family. Goffman (1963) is perhaps the most cited theorist on the issue of stigma in our society. He suggests that "stigma refers to an attribute a person possesses that makes him different from others in the category of persons available for him to be, and of a less desirable kind. He is thus reduced in our minds from a whole and usual person to a tainted, discounted one" (p. 3). There are three kinds of stigma: physical deformities; blemishes of character or behavior such as dishonesty or stealing; and, finally, tribal stigmas, such as race or religion. Suicide would appear to fit the stigma of blemishes of character or behavior.

Goffman's concept of courtesy stigma would seem to apply to the surviving family members. Courtesy stigma is derived from the fact of the relationship to the person who committed suicide. Goffman further suggests that stigmatized individuals can be divided into two broad categories depending upon the type of attribute they possess. First, the "discredited" individual is stigmatized due to an obvious physical handicap or mental impairment. Second, the "discreditable" individual possesses an attribute that has the potential of being stigmatized by others if they become aware of the characteristic. Surely, this embraces the conspiracy of silence that is so often seen when suicide occurs.

A corollary of stigma when applied to suicide is disenfranchised grief. Doka (1989) explains that disenfranchised grief occurs when an individual "experiences a sense of loss but does not have a socially recognized right, role, or capacity to grieve" (p. 3). The person, therefore, suffers a loss, but has little or no opportunity to grieve publicly. The conspiracy of silence thus effectively disenfranchises the griever. As a result, the process of grief is complicated.

Disenfranchisement and stigma are among the major reasons that suicide is considered by many to be the most difficult loss to endure. Others view the suddenness of the death as an important variable.

SUDDEN DEATH

Sudden death is considered to be such a devastating event that it has been termed the "unexpected loss syndrome" (Parkes & Weiss, 1983). The constellation of symptoms characterizing this syndrome are more likely to occur in instances where the death is unexpected. Bereaved survivors have difficulty accepting the reality of the loss, avoid confronting the loss, and are burdened with feelings of self-reproach and despair. With the passage of time, the bereaved remain socially withdrawn, while developing a sense of the continued presence of the dead person, to whom they feel bound. These behaviors do not protect the survivor from loneliness, anxiety, or depression. All persons who experience the loss of a loved one exhibit these reactions, but in the case of sudden death their intensity, duration, and course justifies the label of syndrome.

Sudden or unanticipated death is not limited to suicide, accidents, or murder. Rosen (1990) has suggested that there are three general categories of sudden, unexpected death:

1. Fatal medical events, such as heart attack, stroke, or death during routine surgery.
2. Accidental deaths, such as random accidents or catastrophic events like a natural disaster.
3. Suicide. (p. 98)

The authors of this book would suggest a fourth category to include such things as miscarriage, stillbirth, prenatal death, or Sudden Infant Death Syndrome (SIDS). Although categorically similar to fatal medical events, these tend to be perceived differently by the general public relative to disenfranchised grief (i.e., does the individual have a right to grieve the death).

An underlying idea regarding sudden, unexpected death is that the bereaved would not have time to prepare for the death or go through a period of anticipatory grief. Supposedly, one who has experienced anticipatory grief is better prepared to cope with the final event of death. Typically, this occurs when an elderly person dies or an individual dies following a terminal illness. Overlooked in this belief is that in these two instances the timing of the death still may be unexpected. For example, a person with a terminal illness may be expected to live an additional six months, but might die within days after this prediction is made by the physician. Death, then, would not be expected. Of course, the question can be raised as to how often anyone is prepared for the death of a loved one. This premise does not exclude the idea that one may be more prepared for one death than for another.

In the case of suicide, however, the sudden, perhaps unexpected death is complicated by other factors. Dunne, McIntosh, and Dunne-Maxim (1987) have delineated several factors that are involved when death by suicide occurs. They are:

1. Suicide is usually sudden and unexpected.
2. Suicide is often violent.
3. Suicide engenders guilt in the survivors.
4. Suicide often occurs in systems already experiencing stress.
5. Suicide may lead to harmful expressions of unconscious anger and ultimately to distorted communication patterns.
6. Suicide can compromise usual mourning rituals.
7. Suicide may be followed by withdrawal of usual social supports. (pp. 62–67)

Suicide, therefore, is a sudden death that triggers a number of other processes. Complicating these factors is the specter of social stigma. Other instances of sudden death are probably not affected as greatly by stigma and its constant companion, disenfranchised grief.

What appears to be different about the grief of suicide survivors is that the grief experiences are intensified. Suicide victims are more likely to be plagued by extreme feelings of anger, guilt, abandonment, shame, embarrassment, and a fear of hereditary transmission of the suicide proclivity. The following is a case example of a 43-year-old widow whose husband committed suicide.

> Mrs. H sought professional counseling two years after the suicide of her husband. At the time of the suicide, her husband was age 35 and she was 41; they had one child, a three-year-old son. She sought help to deal with the lingering grief and the enmeshed volatile relationship that existed between her and her, then, five-year-old son. Both are still in family therapy and Mrs. H is also being seen by the same therapist for her unresolved grief issues. Her deceased husband had a Ph.D. and was a professor in a coun-

seling program; Mrs. H had a graduate degree in the same helping discipline and was employed in a mental health agency.

Mr. and Mrs. H had been married 13 years at the time of the suicide. They had decided to adopt a child after it was confirmed that Mrs. H was unable to conceive. They were able to adopt an infant, whom Mr. H cherished. Mr. H had a lengthy history of severe recurrent depression. There was likewise a history of depression in Mr. H's family; two blood relatives had committed suicide. During the marriage Mr. H had received treatment several times for depression. Additionally, Mr. H had an inherited deteriorating eye disorder that would eventually lead to total blindness. Recently, he had been declared legally blind, but rejected the use of visual aids that could improve his limited vision and ability to read. He had been despondent over the recent turn of events.

Two days prior to the suicide, Mr. H had been admitted to a private psychiatric hospital and was worked up to receive Electro-Convulsive-Therapy for the first time. Because of the depth of his despondency, he was placed on suicidal precaution, but apparently this information was not recorded or conveyed properly to the attending staff. One day before the suicide, while in group therapy, Mr. H had been challenged by his psychiatrist, who maintained that he was not suicidal. The day of the suicide, Mr. H had telephoned a friend and told him that he intended to commit suicide that day. The friend believed him to be serious and called Mrs. H at her place of employment and informed her of her husband's intention. Mrs. H believed that if her husband were ever to kill himself it would be by hanging himself with a rope that he kept in the garage of their home. In view of this, Mrs. H did not leave her job to go to the hospital, nor did she call the hospital to alert them.

In spite of Mr. H's suicidal precaution status and his visual impairments, a hospital staff member allowed him a pass to go jogging. Shortly thereafter he was struck by a delivery truck on a nearby street and killed. Some question arose as to whether the death was suicide or accidental and as to the extent to which the hospital was negligent. After some discussion with the church, he received a funeral with a full mass. A subsequent court trial concluded that Mr. H had committed suicide and that the hospital had been negligent.

Mrs. H is a very private person who internalizes her feelings and seldom shows emotion outwardly. This pattern continued after the suicide. She did not allow anyone to see her cry. She suffered sleep disturbance, inability to concentrate, indecisiveness, guilt, increased appetite that led to her gaining about 35 pounds, which was exorbitant considering her diminutive size. It is only recently, four years later, that she has stopped speaking of her deceased husband in the present tense. For the first two years following the death, the living room and the study were kept exactly as they were at the time of the suicide, including the papers on the desk and framed degrees on the wall of the living room. On one occasion, she confided to a close friend that she felt angry at her husband for leaving her to raise their son alone. She and the son have an intensely enmeshed relationship, with neither being able to be out of sight of the other for any appreciable period of time. Mrs. H felt that she had to pursue the court suit against the hospital to ensure her son's financial future and to prove that the hospital was negligent. She has maintained a close relationship with her in-laws and has even relocated to a city where several of them reside.

SUICIDE AND THE LIFE CYCLE

Suicide can occur at any point during the life cycle. Recognition of this fact indicates a need to examine other developmental variables relative to their impact upon the grief process.

Childhood Suicide

Suicide in childhood happens more frequently than generally believed. Medical examiners may not diagnose childhood suicide as such in order to spare the parents or because the State does not require this type of record keeping (Stillion et al., 1989). In spite of the tendency to underreport, the suicide rate for children between the ages of five to 14 in 1986 was 0.8 per 100,000 (U.S. Bureau of the Census, 1987). The most recent figures published (Vital Statistics of the U.S., 1993) are for 1989 and only give data for ages 10 to 14. Suicide rate for this group was 1.4 per 100,000.

Parental grief is generally conceded to be the most severe type of bereavement (see Chapter 3). Suicide would only seem to exacerbate the grief in view of the stigma associated with it. Several studies have reported findings regarding the grief reactions of parents following the suicide of their child. Dunne, McIntosh, and Dunne-Maxim (1987) have summarized these. Included are: (1) stigma; (2) guilt; (3) blame; (4) lack of social support; (5) marital problems and conflicts; and (6) impaired communication (pp. 74–75). The basis of many of these feelings lies in the roles prescribed by society to be undertaken by the responsible parent(s). A child's suicide exposes the parents' perceived incompetence to the world.

Adolescent Suicide

Adolescence, when viewed from a life-span perspective, is thought to be a time of turbulence. It is a time of rapid physical growth and major psychological changes. Adolescents are learning to adjust to a changing physical body, adult sexual feelings, and cognitive changes that allow more complex and abstract configurations and analyses. Considering the difficult tasks that must be accomplished during this relatively brief time span, perhaps it is not surprising that suicide risk is quite high among adolescents. Of the approximately 30,000 documented suicides that are recorded each year, some 5,000 are committed by adolescents. Suicide ranks as the second or third leading cause of death for persons between the ages of 15 and 34. Accidental death is first. Homicide and suicide compete over the years for the number two or three position (Clark, 1993). Over the past several decades, since 1950, the rate has increased so dramatically that Gibson (1989) has described it as being epidemic in proportion. There are some interesting features characteristic of these increases: white males predominate; the growth trend is not restricted to the United States, but is international in scope; and a sizable proportion, about 30%, are adolescents struggling with sexual identity conflicts (Gibson, 1989; Stillion et al., 1989).

Adolescent suicide does not appear to get much national attention unless there is a series of suicides that occur within a brief time span. The media publicizes these, using such terms as *contagion, cluster,* or *copycat*. Some persons believe media reporting of adolescent cluster suicides only serves to increase the likelihood of further suicidal behavior. Local reporting, however, may present problems for the survivors also, in view of the stigma associated with suicidal death.

Suicide severely disrupts the family homeostasis. Parental grief is compounded as a result of the perception that it is a failure on the part of the parents to protect the adolescent against despair so profound that the only solution appeared to be the taking of one's own life. The perfect 20/20 vision of hindsight now allows everyone, including the bereaved, to see clearly all of the previously imperceptible warning signs. Taking on all of the common grief reactions come quite naturally.

Surviving siblings are also affected by the homeostatic disruption. The all-too-frequent communication breakdown adds to the bereavement problems experienced by the siblings. If they are old enough, they may have to undertake the parenting responsibilities for younger siblings for the grieving parents. The parentified sibling is therefore denied the opportunity to grieve. The literature regarding this impact upon siblings is sparse. In fact it is almost nonexistent, and siblings seem to be the forgotten persons.

Suicide in Young and Middle Adulthood

One significant problem arises in the attempt to specify developmental periods in the life span. This problem is the inconsistency and lack of agreement relative to age ranges that identify each period. For example, one writer may define adolescence to include only the teenage years, while another writer may extend the adolescent period to the early twenties. This lack of clarity is even more pronounced when an attempt is made to define middle age and its boundaries between young adulthood and late adulthood. This lack of boundary clarity leads the present authors to combine young adulthood and middlehood into one group. Undeniably, this creates problems, for a 25-year-old undoubtedly will arrive at the decision to commit suicide for different reasons than a 50-year-old.

In examining age groups, one should keep in mind the concept of the "sandwich" generation. These are individuals who are likely to have dependent children as well as aging parents to whom they feel some sense of responsibility. Suicide by a member of this group will profoundly affect three generations. A surviving spouse will be a griever along with children of the suicide victim and one or more parents or parents-in-law. Each generation must deal with the stigma of suicide and the disenfranchised grief. In spite of the larger number of survivors directly affected, this does not ensure greater opportunity for emotional or social support for each other. In fact, it can have the opposite effect because more systems are involved in the family disequilibrium. The spouse has lost a mate, the children have lost an important protector, and the parents of the victim have lost a part of their future. Each survivor mourns the loss of the same person, but it may be for very different reasons.

Suicide and the Elderly

The rate of suicide among elderly people (i.e., 65 and older) is higher than for any other age cohort. Four generalizations have been made regarding the incidence of suicide in the elderly population (Stillion et al., 1989):

1. The elderly are overrepresented among those persons who commit suicide. While comprising about 11% of the population, they account for 17% of the suicides.
2. The attempt-completion rate ratio is higher for the elderly. Among the general population the attempt-completion ratio is estimated to be between 8:1 and 15:1, whereas for persons 65 or older it is 4:1.
3. The ratio of male to female suicides is greater in the elderly population—5:1 versus 3:1 in the total population.
4. The suicide rate among elderly persons is more underreported than in the general population. (p. 165)

Since women tend to outlive men and men are more likely to commit suicide, the surviving spouse in most instances is the widow. Her bereavement, whether from suicide or natural death, signals a significant loss. Her dead spouse may be the only one who remembers her as a sweetheart and bride, shared her highs and lows through such things as pregnancy and childbirth, and knows her intimately. To be abandoned by him through suicide puts her at high risk for complicated grief. Spouses who have been widowed by suicide are themselves at greater risk for suicide (Gibson, 1989; Osterweis et al., 1984). Opportunities for remarriage are fewer for widows than for widowers. One can only speculate as to the extent to which the stigmatization may isolate her even further.

GENDER

Suicide is a white male phenomenon. Males commit suicide three times more frequently than females. Leenaars (1991) has observed that in 1986 there were on the average 66 male and 18 female suicides each day. Suicidology literature is practically void of information relative to the grief impact of suicide contrasting male and female survivors. At this time the knowledge base does not appear to be sufficient to make any definitive statement regarding the impact of gender on the grief response.

RELATIONSHIP TO THE VICTIM

Suicide is not an isolated incident, but rather an event that impacts the entire nuclear and extended family as well as significant others. Family members experience shock, guilt, blame, anger, impotence, anxiety, depression. In other words, this is the symptomatology experienced by most bereaved individuals, but exacerbated by the stigmatizing stance of society. Ambivalence and/or the degree of closeness to the victim affects the nature and intensity of the grief process.

Child survivors of parental suicide are thought to be especially vulnerable. Much of this vulnerability is perhaps affected by three factors: information/communication distortion, guilt, and identification (McIntosh, 1987). In a misconceived attempt to protect the surviving child, no information, distorted information, or false information is often given to the child. This atmosphere of fabrication and/or evasion is a fertile source for the growth of psychological problems. Intense feelings of guilt are likely to emerge. Identification may include taking on the behavior or role of the victim, or it may encompass a belief that one's eventual destiny is also suicide.

McIntosh (1987) has also spoken to the need for information regarding sibling survivor bereavement. There appears to be little to draw from in the literature. Attention tends to be given to parental grief, spousal grief, and child grief of a parent who has suicided. Sibling survivors are the "forgotten mourners." Siblings often assume or inherit responsibility for day-to-day management, thereby postponing their bereavement. The assumption of this level of responsibility does not necessarily lead to a negative outcome, but may prove to be a growth experience for the sibling.

CONCLUSION

Suicide is indeed a complex mode of death that differs in many ways from other types of death. It leaves its indelible mark upon the grieving survivor. Society disenfranchises the grief of the bereaved. Special intervention strategies may be called upon to assist the person who is grieving the victim of suicide. These considerations are discussed in the following chapter.

13

The Treatment of Stigmatized Grief

As established in the previous chapters, the stigma attached to death from suicide or AIDS may deprive the mourner of the socially recognized right, role, or capacity to grieve publicly. This disenfranchisement and stigma can lead to complications in the grief process. It is imperative that therapeutic services be geared toward supplementing the deficiencies in the mourner's repertoire of adaptive strategies. The conspiracy of silence surrounding a stigmatized death leads to destruction of the supportive networks that may have been previously utilized to deal with adversity. Without adequate support, mourners are at risk for complicated bereavement.

THERAPIST-CLIENT RELATIONSHIP

We suggest that the ability of clinicians to deal with stigmatized issues is dependent upon a set of complex transference and countertransference issues. Fear, lack of education and awareness, and personal history all factor into the therapeutic equation. Furthermore, the culpability or the perceived culpability of the deceased and/or the survivors in the death raise sociological, religious, and moral struggles to the forefront. The attitude of the clinician then becomes a primary therapeutic issue. To deal effectively with the surviving family and friends after a stigmatized death, the clinician must assume an attitude that communicates, unequivocally, a nonjudgmental acceptance of the bereaved and must allow for open catharsis within the safety of the therapeutic relationship.

For those who are struggling but willing to attempt the task at hand, a number of approaches may be taken. Education is the first step. The Health Resources and Services Administration (1987) suggests that possession of the appropriate knowledge, attitudes, and skills is the most salient factor in promoting appropriate service delivery to individuals impacted by the AIDS epidemic. In discussing the role of education in the process of overcoming negative attitudes that may impact the therapist–client relationship, Furstenburg and Olson (1984) state: "Preparation . . . is not solely a question of facts, but of helping people to raise consciousness, express and begin to work through their feelings and fears" (p. 56). Riley and Green (1993) found that educational programs for clinicians that offer a psychosocial needs component and an opportunity for values-clarification within an experiential context produced the greatest positive effect on attitude change.

Resolution of the clinician's personal issues related to suicide or AIDS is an essential component in a healthy therapeutic relationship. A therapist who has unresolved anger over a relative who committed suicide or who holds strong religious convictions about the morality of such an act may inadvertently confound the therapeutic relationship with these issues, further ostracizing the client. Other clinicians may be unsuccessful in their efforts to transform their judgmental attitudes regarding the mode of death, the deceased, or the survivors. In these situations, an appropriate referral to a therapist who can render these services in a nonjudgmental manner is certainly warranted. In the words of Geis & Fuller, (1986):

> In any given era, we might be the wrong age, sex, skin color, or religion, but we may also be in the wrong state of physical, emotional or financial health. As individuals who might find ourselves among the unwanted, how do we wish our society (or our therapeutic counterparts) to respond? (p. 40)

The ability to provide adequate psychosocial support and intervention to the bereaved after a stigmatized death is dependent upon the clinician's ability to compassionately and appropriately respond to this question. Through this personal exploration, the therapist-client relationship then becomes the basis for building a positive, nurturing support system.

TREATMENT PLANNING

Uncomplicated grief is the normal psychological reaction to the death of a loved one. As discussed throughout this book, the bereavement response has an instinctual component, though mourning behaviors may have a cultural influence. After a stigmatized death, however, survivors may be denied the usual means of mourning due to social isolation and withdrawal. Since grief is a reactive phenomenon rather than a problem created by inadequate problem solving or interpersonal conflict, a supportive approach to counseling should initially be employed. Supportive counseling techniques are designed to build upon the client's existing strengths. Defenses are generally left in place, and the focus of counseling shifts from the past to the present. This approach is indicated for those who are in crisis and who have limited internal or external resources.

On the other end of the continuum are exploratory methods. Exploratory counseling focuses on antecedents to the presenting problem, prior unresolved conflict, and developmental concerns. While presenting problems are not ignored, they are generally viewed as part of the client's lifetime pattern.

Although very different, supportive and exploratory methods are inevitably combined throughout the course of therapy. A client in crisis initially needs supportive counseling and may resist or prematurely terminate the counseling process if the clinician shifts to exploratory methods too early in the counseling process. However, once the initial crisis is stabilized, exploratory methods may be introduced gradually, as indicated.

The dimensions of stigmatized grief have been defined in terms of affective, cognitive, behavioral, and physiological symptomatology. Clinical interventions should be integrated, addressing each aspect of the grief reaction.

The expression of emotion can be most difficult after a stigmatized death. The bereaved may repress or deny their feelings due to conflicting emotions about the deceased. For example, a parent who has lost an adult child to AIDS may feel tremendous guilt over past interpersonal conflicts. A parent who has lost a child to suicide may have coexisting feelings of anger at the child for committing such an act and a sense of overwhelming loss. Estranged relationships provide ambiguous definitions of appropriate mourning behavior. Therefore, an affective focus can be beneficial in sorting through, validating, and allowing for the expression of these conflicting emotions within a supportive context. This process is generally expedited by combining other methods (i.e., replacing irrational thoughts, increasing pleasurable activities).

Cognitive interventions should focus on reframing irrational and self-destructive thoughts. Clients may verbalize thoughts such as: "My mother committed suicide, so it is my fate as well," or "If I had been a better parent my child would not have been gay, and therefore, would not have gotten AIDS." Counselors can detect irrational or inaccurate thought processes and assist clients in replacing them with more healthy cognitions.

Behavioral approaches are effective in ameliorating disorders such as phobias or substance abuse problems. Mourners who have faced difficult social situations due to the mode of death may shun all social contact and develop a phobic fear of social interactions. Others may turn to alcohol or drugs as a way of coping with their grief in the absence of normally supportive social structures. Though behavioral approaches have proven effective at reducing or eliminating undesirable behavior, these methods used alone may be ineffective in dealing with the initial cause of the problem (e.g., irrational thoughts or overwhelming levels of affect).

Physiological symptomatology such as insomnia or cardiovascular changes are inherent in the bereavement process, but can be exacerbated with the onset of PTSD or other psychological complications. When addressing the physiological component, a medical doctor (preferably a psychiatrist) should be consulted. The functional level of the client should always be considered. A disturbance of sleep, appetite, or other physiological processes should be considered a normative part of the post-death reaction. Medications are indicated when the symptomatology seriously impairs the client's ability to function and is prolonged in nature. Medical interventions should be performed in conjunction with other cognitive, behavioral, or affective approaches to increase efficacy.

Essential to treatment planning is determining who will be involved in the counseling process. The literature documents the importance of a combination of group and individual processes to provide the appropriate intrapersonal and interpersonal support and exploration necessary to the survivors following a death from AIDS or suicide (Appel & Wrobleski, 1987; Fuller et al., 1988). Though the exact combination of modalities and the appropriate timing of their introduction should be dependent upon a thorough assessment, these authors propose that individual therapy, in combination with other supportive or therapeutic services, is indicated in the majority of the cases due to the alienation and stigma associated with the loss. The following discussions will outline the components of these modalities that are important for successful service delivery.

TREATMENT CONSIDERATIONS

Professional intervention is needed for some survivors, while self-help services may be sufficient for others. The need for professional intervention may be limited to "psychological first aid" at the beginning of the crisis period. Others may need assistance after they have struggled with their bereavement for a protracted period of time during which they utilized other support with minimal success. Others who have not developed more mature coping strategies may require more long-term psychotherapy.

It is an absolute necessity that the therapist have sufficient knowledge to distinguish between normal and pathological forms of grief within the context of the stigmatized grief model. The following discussions will explore assessment considerations as well as professional and self-help intervention applications.

Phase I—Establish Rapport

As discussed earlier, the therapist-client relationship is a critical variable in determining treatment outcome. Due to the stigma attached to the loss, the mourner may not reach out for assistance for fear of being judged or ostracized. A compassionate, nonjudgmental atmosphere is the only basis for establishing trust between the client and the clinician. Normalization of the mourner's emotional experience allows for emotional expression and affective acknowledgment of the loss. The clinician must take care not to rush the client and should respect the stages or phases of grief that are represented throughout the bereavement process.

Many survivors will have tragic experiences to report (e.g., finding the body of the deceased after a fatal gunshot, seeing the physical and emotional deterioration of their loved one from AIDS), many of which will be distressing to the clinician to hear. It is important that this reaction not be expressed in a manner that discourages future discussions of this experience. Mourners may need to discuss the issue repeatedly as a means of processing and resolving feelings regarding the event. They should not have the additional burden of protecting the clinician from distressing details. These transference and countertransference issues must be closely monitored so as to engage clients long enough to perform a thorough assessment.

Phase II—Determine the Client's Adaptive Capacities

The analysis of psychological variables is necessary to uncover information on the impact of loss on the survivor, the urgency of the situation, and the client's receptivity to counseling. This assessment should be performed within the context of a social, economic, and cultural framework so as to determine the normative patterns with which to compare the client's coping strategies. Clinicians who are unfamiliar with the cultural norms within the survivor's community should seek the appropriate consultation and/or review the literature for the necessary information.

Of particular concern to clinicians is the assessment of lethality in survivors following a death from suicide or AIDS. Both of these deaths carry an increased incidence of suicide in the survivors. Several explanations can be offered for this phenomenon: a learned response to adversity (after a suicide); a fear of physical suffering like that witnessed in the deceased (especially for those survivors who have been diagnosed as HIV positive); or the feeling that suicide is a family legacy. The most effective method for dealing with this issue is to be direct and specific in the assessment of lethality.

Many clinicians fear directly questioning a client about suicidal intent for fear of unknowingly suggesting such an act or communicating a lack of confidence in the client's ability to cope. A compassionate and honest approach to assessment of a client's potential for self-destructive behavior communicates an expectation and assumption of trust, while modeling appropriate communication patterns. Most suicidal clients provide some warning of their intent, are ambivalent or conflicted about their decision, and can be redirected via immediate intervention. Failure to address this issue, especially with this high-risk population, is injudicious at best.

An assessment of a client's potential lethality should contain the following elements:

1. *An exploration of historical factors.* Not only does familial history of suicide (especially maternal suicide) play a role in suicide patterns among the survivors, the mourner's own previous coping patterns must be explored. Survivors who have a history of suicide attempts, gestures, or plans should be considered as extremely high risk.
2. *Assessment of patterns of affective response.* Depression, hopelessness, and helplessness are all associated with suicidal ideation. A mourner with overwhelming levels of affect may experience suicidal thoughts as a means of escaping the pain. However, many mourners may experience self-destructive thoughts as their mood begins to improve

and their energy level increases. Too often, this is when clinicians may feel the client is "out of the woods" and may discontinue close monitoring of the client's potential lethality.

3. *Assessment of the underlying motivation for contemplating suicide.* Clients who express suicidal ideation are motivated by a number of factors: to end their suffering; as a self-fulfilling prophesy; to punish others; to gain attention, etc. Understanding the underlying need can provide the clinician with the necessary direction to develop alternative strategies for fulfilling the client's needs.

4. *Identification of the duration of the suicidal ideation.* Most grief-related suicidal ideation is brief in nature and is usually associated with the emotional expression and depressive stages of grief. Hipple and Crombolic (1979) suggest that although suicidal ideation is severe at the onset, it should subside within six weeks. Due to the nature and duration of stigmatized grief, the clinician should not be surprised by a recurrence of this phenomenon over time and should be constantly monitoring the survivor's current status.

5. *Existence of a plan and availability of the means.* A client who has formulated a plan to commit suicide, and who has obtained the means (or could easily obtain the means) for carrying out this plan should be considered at very high risk. Clients who fall into this category are considered likely candidates for inpatient stabilization.

6. *The exploration of substance usage.* A survivor in crisis who has a history of substance abuse or dependence and who has voiced suicidal intent or ideation should be considered unpredictable and untrustworthy as long as he or she is abusing substances. A "no suicide" contract agreed upon by a sober client may be meaningless once the client is under the influence of a substance. Controlling the substance use is of primary importance for successful outpatient treatment.

All assessments should include a mental status exam as a routine part of the evaluation process. Due to the nature of the loss and the ensuing emotional turmoil, normally high-functioning clients may experience symptomatology consistent with a brief psychotic disorder. The DSM-IV (APA, 1994) describes this response as at least one of the following positive psychotic symptoms: "delusions, hallucinations, disorganized speech (e.g., frequent derailment or incoherence) or grossly disorganized or catatonic behavior" (p. 302). An associated feature of this disorder is suicidal or aggressive behavior. Although a sudden onset of the disorder is common, the individual usually returns to premorbid functioning within one month.

Other psychiatric conditions such as mood disorders or anxiety disorders can coexist and confound the grief process. A careful examination of these variables and an accurate diagnosis should be made for successful treatment.

Suicide and AIDS-related deaths are losses that impact entire family and social systems. Clinicians should look for dysfunctional interaction patterns that may prove counterproductive to the recovery of the individual. Unfinished business, unresolved interpersonal conflict, and emotional cutoffs are all problems common to survivors after a stigmatized death. An assessment of family and social system strengths, weaknesses, and resources are mandatory to productive intervention.

Phase III—Intervention Strategies

Some general, practical rules apply when working with individuals suffering from stigmatized grief. The following is a summary of some essential elements.

1. With permission, do not be afraid to touch. Survivors may feel dirty and rejected because of the nature of the death (especially AIDS).
2. Ask about the death and be prepared to listen. Initially, the clinician may be the mourner's only source of support.
3. Support decision making.
4. Keep any promises made. Trust may be difficult to obtain and keep.
5. Be prepared for expressions of anger.
6. Set realistic expectations for what the survivor can accomplish. It is important not to set the client up to fail.
7. Support hope for the future.

Survivors who have lost a loved one to AIDS or suicide may feel they have lost some control over their life and may feel victimized by the stigma attached to the death. Therefore, it is important for the clinician to empower the client whenever possible by providing and allowing for choices, establishing achievable goals, and normalizing the grief experience. Collaboratively determining treatment goals is one method of empowering the client. Although the mourner may simply want to feel better or survive, it is essential that the clinician respond to the client in a manner that is consistent with the client's capacities, being careful not to push too hard or expect too much. Some examples of treatment goals with this population are as follows:

1. Provide education about the stigmatized grief process—what to expect, danger signs, etc.—by providing reference books on stigmatized

grief and by reviewing symptomatology relative to this mode of death.

2. Explore the secrets associated with the death by assisting the client in satisfactorily answering the following questions: Whom should I tell? Who should not know? How will I handle it when _____ finds out? Clinicians can assist the client in dealing with these issues by assisting in the development of communication strategies and by offering to educate family, friends, or others in the survivor's natural support system. Individuals are usually not as frightened by something they understand or have had an opportunity to discuss.

Although exposing secrets may prove beneficial to some by alleviating social support tension, the cost of exposing the circumstances surrounding the death may be high for others. Some members of the system may be unable to compassionately deal with the news and may be a destructive force in the system. It is advisable to explore the cost of secrecy with the client and teach healthy problem-solving strategies so the client can most effectively make these decisions.

3. Initiate healing by teaching techniques such as relaxation, healthy communication strategies, and disputing irrational thoughts in and out of the counseling session. It is important that the client have the opportunity to integrate these methods in real-life situations. Homework assignments allow for this practical application and offer the clinician and the client the opportunity to modify these approaches as needed to fit the client's life circumstance.

4. Assist the client (or the family) in identifying at least five positive aspects of their relationship with the deceased to help them gain motivation, self-confidence, and hope for dealing with current problems.

5. Supplement appropriate mourning rituals or ceremonies. Grief is a collective experience, and clinicians should encourage a systemic response via mourning rituals. As discussed in the previous chapters on AIDS-related grief and grief following a suicide, survivors are often deprived of the right to adequately mourn the deceased due to a lack of access to or the absence of the rituals and customs associated with bereavement. The clinician can supplement this process by sending a sympathy card, encouraging the survivor to assemble a small but meaningful ceremony where the survivors can pay their last respects, and/or assisting the client in writing a eulogy (as appropriate).

6. Increase social support resources by identifying and attending at least one AIDS bereavement or suicide survivors' group within the next 30 days. Depending on the individual's existing supportive network

and personal strengths or weaknesses, self-help groups may or may not be beneficial. Appel and Wrobleski (1987), after an extensive review of the literature, have summarized why self-help groups are thought to be beneficial. They provide an opportunity for the following experiences:

- Personal interaction based on a common identification or shared status. Since the stigma and disenfranchisement associated with suicide or AIDS robs the survivor of mourner status, this is particularly important.
- Education to the survivor about the group's common problem.
- Allows the mourner to receive help with little or no out-of-pocket expense. Many survivors may experience financial difficulties as a result of the death due to a failure of insurance to pay because of the type of death, the legal status (or lack thereof) of the survivor, familial conflict, absence of a will, etc.
- An atmosphere where the survivor can feel cared about and supported.
- A normalization of feelings by allowing the mourner the opportunity to discover that others have experienced the same feelings.
- Learn new coping strategies from those who have experienced the same issues.
- Allows for positive reinforcement, which helps maintain change.
- Allows the survivor to engage in collective advocacy for social change.
- Allows the mourner the benefit of being a helper for someone else.

It is for these reasons that there has been a proliferation of mutual aid groups within the past two decades. Specific information on how to access AIDS bereavement and suicide survivors' groups can be found in the Appendix.

Treatment goals should always be stated in measurable terms so that the clinician and the client can evaluate progress and build upon successful completion of goals. As always, the goals should be time limited, driven by the client's desire for completion, with input from the clinician on reasonable expectations.

Dunne-Maxin (1987) has delineated the recurring clinical themes that may arise in the course of therapy with a client suffering from stigmatized grief. They are:

1. The persistent question of why.
2. Whether irrational or appropriate, survivors experience inexorable guilt.

3. The alteration of social relationships as a consequence of real or imagined stigma.
4. The course of grief is complex and likely to be incomplete.
5. Due to the social isolation and the nature of the death, suicide may begin to be seen as a solution to problems.
6. The stigma and mode of death may impact a survivor's capacity to trust others.

Phase IV—Termination

The process of grief is generally considered complete when the client begins to reinvest in emotional relationships and pleasurable activities. However, as with other forms of bereavement, there may be a "waxing and waning" of symptoms over time (Bard & Sangrey, 1987). Clients may choose to discontinue treatment because they are experiencing a reduction of grief-related symptoms only to reexperience overwhelming emotions at specific times (usually special occasions like birthdays, anniversaries, etc.). Clients should be warned this may occur and be given permission to return to counseling for support as needed.

CONCLUSION

The treatment of stigmatized grief is confounded by the mode of death and by the stigma that pervades societal perceptions of the deceased and of the survivors. Intervention should be provided by clinicians who have a good understanding of the dynamic of this type of bereavement and who have resolved personal issues related to AIDS and suicide. Stigmatized grief differs from traumatic grief in the development of symptomatology but carries with it an ecological component that makes it a unique phenomenon, distinct from normative and traumatic grief processes.

Conclusion: The Many Faces of Bereavement

Bereavement does in fact have many faces. Until approximately two decades ago the process of bereavement tended to be seen in a rather narrowly focused manner. Bereaved persons were expected to grieve in essentially the same way, with the societal expectations not taking into account their relationship to the deceased nor the manner of death. All bereaved persons were expected to grieve like an older adult who had lost a lifelong spouse. Generally it was expected that if the deceased had been ill for a sufficiently long period, the survivor would have had time to engage in some degree of anticipatory grief. Some allowance was made if the death was a sudden and unexpected occurrence following such incidents as heart attack or stroke.

Acceptance of the stage models of grief reinforced our beliefs about what constituted "normal" bereavement. When the bereaved deviated too much from this pattern or appeared to be grieving for too long, their grieving was thought to be pathological. As a consequence, many persons were mislabeled and treated improperly.

This book has sought to dispel these myths and demonstrate that grieving is an individual journey that is influenced by multiple factors such as the manner of death, ages of the deceased and the survivor, nature of the relationship between the survivor and the deceased, and whether or not the death is stigmatized. When bereavement is examined from this broader perspective, it facilitates the understanding of the variability of grief experienced and how it is exhibited by different persons. Emphasis in this book is upon death that is perceived as being other than "natural."

In Section I the chapter on Parental Grief discusses the devastating

181

impact the loss of a child has upon parents. Foremost among the factors that cause this severe grief response are (1) the parents' belief that they should be able to protect their children from any type of threat or harm; (2) the expectation that the old should die first; and (3) the parental hopes for the future of the child have been destroyed.

Section II, Traumatic Grief, addresses murder and vehicular homicide. We also explore the grief response following death as a consequence of a large-scale community disaster or critical incident. These types of death are so overwhelming that the subsequent grief response often warrants an evaluation within the Post-traumatic Stress Disorder (PTSD) framework. Assessment and intervention require insights and strategies that may differ markedly from those utilized in situations where the death occurred due to prolonged illness.

Stigmatized Death is considered in Section III, specifically the grief response following suicidal death and AIDS-related death. Survivors must deal not only with the usual pain experienced during bereavement, but also with disenfranchised grief because of death caused by nonsanctioned social behavior or perceived culpability. As a result, the bereaved may be forced to grieve in solitary silence.

Although one may be wont to say that death is death and bereavement is bereavement, we argue that there are in fact significant differences in grief responses. What may seem as a pathological response may in fact be normal considering the circumstances of the death. There is, however, considerable overlap in the presenting symptomatology of grief following the various modes of death. Special attention, therefore, needs to be paid to the dynamics that appear to have triggered the symptom. A case in point is stigmatized grief. Shame, guilt, and self-denigration may present as an integral part of the grief experience following several modes of death, but one could easily surmise that these feelings would be much more intense if the death were stigmatized.

The future is indeed promising. As we learn more about the differential impact of bereavement, more effective intervention strategies can be developed. Intervention personnel can be used differentially according to their levels of expertise and the needs of the bereaved person.

Advances in thanatological research has also made promising progress within the past few years. The utilization of longitudinal research designs has added to the bereavement knowledge base. For example, it is now possible to state with certainty that earlier beliefs about the short duration of the grief period were totally erroneous. Longitudinal study designs have also made it possible to account for changes over time. There is no longer reliance upon simplistic measures of central tendency and percentages, but there is more utilization of sophisticated procedures such as multiple regression and path analysis. Another positive sign is the increasing numbers of persons who are selecting bereavement research as an area of study. Also, several professional publications are devoted to bereavement issues and many journals seem willing to publish materials on death and dying.

Bereavement is indeed an emerging field of scientific study. Knowledge is being generated by survivors who assist with their "how to" publications and presentations. Coupled with this is the dissemination of information by clinicians and researchers. This combination of efforts is promising.

Appendix: Organizations for Survivors and Victims

AIDS Hotline 800-342-AIDS/2432
AIDS Hotline (Deaf/TTY) 800-243-7889
AIDS Hotline (Spanish Speaking) 800-344-SIDA/7437
AIDS Hotline for Teens 800-234-8336

Compassionate Friends 708-990-0010

Grief Recovery Hotline 800-445-4808

Heartbeat (for those who lost a loved one to suicide) . . . 719-596-2575

Mothers Against Drunk Driving (MADD) 800-438-6233

National Hospice Link 800-331-1620
National Organization for Victim Assistance 800-879-6682
National Survivors of Suicide 414-442-4638
National Victims Center 800-394-2255
National Victims Resource Center 800-627-6872

Ray of Hope (for those who lost a loved
    one to suicide) 319-337-9890

Sudden Infant Death Syndrome Foundation
    (SIDS) 800-221-SIDS/7437

References

Adams, D. W., & Deveau, E. J. (1986). Helping dying adolescents: Needs and responses. In C. A. Corr & J. N. McNeil (Eds.), *Adolescence and death.* pp. 79–96. New York: Springer.

Adler, A. (1943). Neuropsychiatric complications in victims of Boston's Coconut Grove disaster. *Journal of the American Medical Association, 123,* 1098–1101.

Albert, E. (1986). Illness and deviance: The response of the press to AIDS. In D. A. Feldman & T. M. Johnson (Eds.), *The social dimensions of AIDS: Methods and therapy.* pp. 163–178. New York: Praeger.

Aldrich, C. K. (1963). The dying patient's grief. *Journal of the American Medical Association, 184,* 329–331.

American Psychiatric Association. (1994). *Diagnostic and statistical manual of mental disorders* (4th ed.). Washington, DC: American Psychiatric Association.

Amick-McMullan, A., Kilpatrick, D. G., Veronen, L. J., & Smith, S. (1989, January). Family survivors of homicide victims: Theoretical perspectives and an exploratory study. *Journal of Traumatic Stress, 2*(1), 21–33.

Appel, Y. H., & Wrobleski, A. (1987). Self-help and support groups: Mutual aid for survivors. In E. J. Dunne, J. L. McIntosh, & K. Dunne-Maxin (Eds.), *Suicide and its aftermath.* pp. 215–233. New York: W. W. Norton.

Badenhorst, J. C. C., & Van Schalkwyk, S. J. (1992). Minimizing post-traumatic stress in critical mining incidents. *Employee Assistance Quarterly, 7*(3), 79–89.

Bard, M., & Sangrey, D. (1986). *The crime victim's book.* New York: Brunner/Mazel.

Bardis, P. D. (1961). A Religion Scale. *Social Science, 36*(2), 121–123.

Batchelor, W. F. (1984). AIDS: A public health and psychological emergency. *American Psychologist, 39*(1), 1283.

Bergeron, J. P., & Handley, P. R. (1992). Bibliography on AIDS–related bereavement and grief. *Death Studies, 16,* 247–267.

Bornstein, P. E., & Clayton, P. J. (1972). The anniversary reaction. *Diseases of the Nervous System, 33,* 470–472.

Bowlby, J. (1973). *Attachment and loss: Separation (Vol. II).* New York: Basic Books.

Bowman, N. J. (1980). *Differential reactions to dissimilar types of death: Specifically the homicide/murder.* Unpublished doctoral dissertation, United States International University, San Diego, CA.

Bravo, M., Rubio-Stipec, M., Canino, G. J., Woodbury, M. A., & Ribera, J. C. (1990). The psychological sequela of disaster stress prospectively and retrospectively evaluated. *American Journal of Community Psychology, 18,* 661–680.

Bromet, E., & Dunn, L. (1981). Mental health of mothers nine months after the Three Mile Island accident. *Urban and Social Change Review, 14,* 12–15.

Brookmeyer, R. (1991). Reconstruction and future trends of the AIDS epidemic in the United States. *Science, 253,* 37–42.

Bureau of Justice Statistics. (1988, February). In Lawrence A. Greenfeld (Ed.), *Special report: "Drunk driving."* U.S. Department of Justice, NCJ-109945.

Burgess, A. W. (1975). Family reaction to homicide. *American Journal of Orthopsychiatry, 45,* 391–398.

Burgess, A. W., & Holstrom, L. (1974). Rape trauma syndrome. *American Journal of Psychiatry, 131,* 981–986.

Cain, A. C. (Ed.). (1972). *Survivors of suicide.* Springfield, IL: Charles C. Thomas.

Caserta, M. S., Van Pelt, J., & Lund, D. A. (1989). Advice on the adjustment to loss from bereaved older adults: An examination of resources and outcomes. In D. A. Lund (Ed.), *Older bereaved spouses.* pp. 123–134. New York: Hemisphere Publishing.

Centers for Disease Control and Prevention. (1994). Estimates of HIV prevalence and projected AIDS cases. *Morbidity and Mortality Weekly Report, 39,* 110–119.

Clark, D. C. (1993). Suicidal behavior in childhood and adolescence: Recent studies and clinical implications. *Psychiatric Annals, 23*(5), 271–283.

Colt, G. W. (1991). *The enigma of suicide.* New York: Summit Books.

Cook, J. A., & Wimberly, D. W. (1983). If I should die before I wake: Religious commitment and adjustment to the death of a child. *Journal for Scientific Study of Religion 22*(3), 222–238.

Cugley, J. M., & Savage, R. D. (1984). Cognitive impairment and personality adjustment in Vietnam veterans. *Australian Psychologist, 19,* 205–216.

Davidson, G. (1979). *Understanding: Death of the wished-for child.* Springfield, IL: OGR Service Corp.

Davis, L. V. (1986). Role theory. In F. J. Turner (Ed.), *Social work treatment: Interlocking theoretical approaches* (3rd ed.). pp. 541–564. New York: The Free Press.

Dershimer, R. A. (1990). *Counseling the bereaved.* New York: Pergamon Press.

Doka, K. J. (1989). *Disenfranchised grief: Recognizing hidden sorrow.* Lexington, MA: Lexington Books.

Douglas, J. D. (1990). Patterns of change following parent death in midlife adults. *Omega, 22*(2), 123–137.

Doyle, P. (1980). *Grief counseling and sudden death.* Springfield, IL: Charles C. Thomas.

Dunne, E. J., McIntosh, J. L., & Dunne-Maxim, K. (1987). *Suicide and its aftermath.* New York: W. W. Norton.

Dunne-Maxim, K. (1987). Survivors and the media. Pitfalls and potentials. In E. J. Dunne, J. L. McIntosh, & K. Dunne-Maxin (Eds.), *Suicide and its aftermath.* pp. 45–56. New York: W. W. Norton.

Engle, G. L. (1961). Is grief a disease? A challenge for medical research. *Psychosomatic Medicine, 23,* 18–22.

Erikson, K. T. (1976). *Everything in its path: The destruction of community in the Buffalo Creek flood.* New York: Simon & Schuster.

Farberow, N. L. (1991). Adult survivors after suicide: Research problems and needs. In A. A. Leenaars (Ed.), *Life span perspectives of suicide*. New York: Plenum Press.

Faschingbauer, T. R., Devaul, R. A., & Zisook, S. (1977). Development of the Texas Inventory of Grief. *American Journal of Psychiatry, 134*, 696–698.

Federal Bureau of Investigation. *Crime in the United States—1990*. (1991). FBI Uniform Crime Reporting Section. Washington, DC: U.S. Government Printing Office.

Fish, W. C. (1986). Differences in grief intensity in bereaved parents. In T. A. Rando (Ed.), *Parental loss of a child*. pp. 415–428. Champaign, IL: Research Press.

Flannery, R. (1987). *Working with traumatized populations through group psychotherapy*. Paper presented at the 3rd annual meeting of the International Society of Traumatic Stress Studies, Dallas, TX.

Folta, J., & Deck, G. (1976). Grief, the funeral, and the friend. In V. Pine, A. H. Kutscher, D. Peretz, R. C. Slater, R. DeBellis, A. I. Volk, & D. J. Cherico (Eds.), *Acute grief and the funeral*. Springfield, IL: Charles C. Thomas.

Foster, D. J., O'Malley, J. E., & Koocher, G. P. (1981). The parent interviews. In G. P. Koocher & J. E. O'Malley (Eds.), *The Damocles syndrome: Psychosocial consequences of surviving childhood cancer*. pp. 86–100. New York: McGraw-Hill.

Freud, S. (1920). Beyond the pleasure principle. In *Complete psychological works* (standard ed., Vol. 18). Translated and edited by J. Strachey. London: Hogarth Press, 1959.

Frolkey, C. A. (1992, May–June). Critical incidents and traumatic events: The differences. *EAP Digest, 12*(4), 35–37.

Fuller, R. L., & Geis, S. B. (1985). Communicating with the grieving family. *Journal of Family Practice, 21*, 139–144.

Fuller, R. L, Geis, S. B., & Rush, J. (1988). Lovers of AIDS victims: A minority experience. *Death Studies, 12*, 17.

Furstenburg, A., & Olson, M. (1984). Social work and AIDS. *Social Work in Health Care, 9*(4), 45–62.

Gardiner, A., & Pritchard, M. (1977). Mourning, mummification, and living with the dead. *British Journal of Psychiatry, 130*, 23–28.

Geis, S. B., & Fuller, R. L. (1986). Lovers of AIDS victims: Psychosocial stresses and counseling needs. *Death Studies, 10*, 43–53.

Gibson, P. (1989). Gay male, lesbian youth suicide. In M. R. Feinleib (Ed.), *Report of the secretary's task force on youth suicide*. Washington, DC: U.S. Government Printing Office.

Gillis, E. (1986). A single parent: Confronting the loss of an only child. In T. A. Rando (Ed.), *Parental loss of a child*. pp. 315–320. Champaign, IL: Research Press.

Gleser, G. C., Green, B. L., & Winget, C. (1981). *Prolonged psychosocial effects of disaster: A study of Buffalo Creek*. New York: Academic Press.

Goffman, E. (1963). *Stigma: Notes on the management of spoiled identity*. New York: Simon & Schuster.

Golan, N. (1978). *Treatment in crisis situations*. New York: The Free Press.

Goodgame, R. W. (1990). Aids in Uganda—Clinical and social features. *New England Journal of Medicine, 323*, 383–389.

Gorer, G. D. (1965). *Death, grief, and mourning*. New York: Doubleday.

Green, B. L., Grace, M. C., & Gleser, G. C. (1985). Identifying survivors at risk: Long-term impairment following the Beverly Hills Supper Club fire. *Journal of Consulting and Clinical Psychology, 53*, 672–678.

Guilford, J. P., & Fruchter, B. (1978). *Fundamental statistics in psychology and education.* New York: McGraw-Hill.

Harris, J., Sprang, G., & Komsak, K. (1987). *This could never happen to me.* Criminal Justice Division, Office of the Governor (Texas).

Health Resources and Services Administration, U.S. Public Health Service. (1987). *Proceedings of multidisciplinary curriculum development conference on HIV infection.* Washington, DC: U.S. Government Printing Office.

Helzer, J. E., Robins, L. N., & McEvoy, L. (1987). Post-traumatic stress disorder in the general population: Findings of the Epidemiologic Catchment Area Survey. *New England Journal of Medicine, 317*, 1630–1634.

Hepworth, D. H., & Larsen, J. A. (1993). *Direct social work practice: Theory and skills* (4th ed.). Belmont, CA: Wadsworth.

Herek, G. M., & Glunt, E. K. (1991). AIDS-related attitudes in the United States: A preliminary conceptualization. *Journal of Sex Research, 28*(1), 99–123.

Hickey, T., & Szabo, K. (1973). Grief intervention and the helping professional. In T. Hickey (Ed.), *Grief: Its recognition and resolution.* University Park, PA: Penn State University Press.

Hillenberg, J. B., & Wolf, K. L. (1988). Psychological impact of traumatic events: Implications for employee assistance intervention. *Employee Assistance Quarterly, 4*(2), 1–11.

Hipple, J., & Crombolic, P. (1979). *The counselor and suicidal crisis.* Springfield, IL: Charles C. Thomas.

Holmes, R. H., & Rahe, R. H. (1967). The Social Adjustment Rating Scale. *Journal of Psychosomatic Research, 11*, 213–218.

Hooyman, N. R., & Kiyak, H. R. (1993). *Social gerontology: A multidisciplinary perspective.* Boston: Allyn & Bacon.

Horowitz, M. J., Daniel, S. W., Krupnick, J., Marmar, C., Wilner, N., & DeWitt, K. (1984). Reactions to the death of a parent. *Journal of Nervous and Mental Disease, 172*(4), 383–392.

Horowitz, M. J., Wiloner, N., & Alvarez, W. (1979). Impact of Events Scale: A measure of subjective stress. *Psychosomatic Medicine, 41*, 209–218.

Ingram, R. E. (1986). *Information processing approaches to clinical psychology.* New York: Academic Press.

Kalish, R. A., & Reynolds, D. K. (1976). *Death and ethnicity: A psychocultural study.* Los Angeles: University of Southern California Press.

Kamerman, J. B. (1988). *Death in the midst of life: Social and cultural influences on death, grief, and mourning.* Englewood Cliffs, NJ: Prentice-Hall.

Kaniasty, K. Z., Norris, F. H., & Murrell, S. A. (1990). Received and perceived social support following a natural disaster. *Journal of Applied Social Psychology, 20*, 85–114.

Kaplan, D. M., Grobstein, R., & Smith, A. (1976). Predicting the impact of severe illness in families. *Health and Social Work, 1*(3), 71–82.

Kardiner, A. (1941). *The traumatic neurosis of war.* New York: Hoeber Press.

Kastenbaum, R. (1972). *The psychology of death.* New York: Springer.

Kastenbaum, R., & Aisenberg, R. (1976). *The psychology of death.* New York: Springer.

Keane, T. M., Caddell, J. M., & Taylor, K. L. (1988). Mississippi scale for post-traumatic stress disorder: Three studies in reliability and validity. *Journal of Consulting and Clinical Psychology, 56,* 85–90.

Keane, T. M., Malloy, P. F., & Fairbanks, J. A. (1984). PTSD: Evidence for diagnostic validity and methods of psychological assessment. *Journal of Clinical Psychology, 43,* 32–43.

Keane, T. M., Wolfe, J., & Taylor, K. L. (1987). PTSD: Evidence for diagnostic validity and methods of psychological assessment. *Journal of Clinical Psychology, 43,* 32–43.

Kerlinger, F. N., & Pedhauzer, E. J. (1973). *Multiple regression in behavior research.* New York: Holt, Rinehart & Winston.

Kilijanek, T. S., & Drabek, T. E. (1979). Assessing long-term impacts of a natural disaster: A focus on the elderly. *Gerontologist, 19,* 555–566.

Kilpatrick, D. G., Veronen, L., Saunders, B. E., Best, C. L., Amick-McMullan, A., & Paduhovich, J. (1987). *Psychological impact of crime: A study of randomly surveyed crime victims, final report.* National Institute of Justice Grant 84-IJ-CX-0039. Washington, DC: National Institute of Justice.

Klass, D. (1988). *Parental grief: Solace and resolution.* New York: Springer.

Koehler, L. (1990). But it's been over a year: A profile of parental bereavement after the first year. *Social Work Perspective, 1,* 41–45.

Krause, N. (1987, Summer). Exploring the impact of a natural disaster on the health and well-being of older adults. *Journal of Human Stress,* 61–69.

Kübler-Ross, E. (1969). *On death and dying.* New York: Macmillan.

Kulka, R. A., Schlenger, W. E., Fairbanks, J. A., Hough, R. L., Jordon, B. K., Marmar, C. R., & Weiss, D. S. (1988). *National Vietnam veterans readjustment study advance report: Preliminary findings from the National Survey of the Vietnam Generations.* Executive summary. Washington, DC: Veterans Administration.

Kulka, R. A., Schlenger, W. E., Fairbanks, J. A., Hough, R. L., Jordan, B. K., Marmar, C. R., & Weiss, D.S. (1990). *Trauma and the Vietnam War generation.* New York: Brunner/Mazel.

Kupst, M. J. (1986). Death of a child from serious illness. In T. A. Rando (Ed.), *Parental loss of a child.* pp. 191–200. Champaign, IL: Research Press.

Kushner, H. (1981). *When bad things happen to good people.* New York: Shocken Books.

Lang, A., & Gottlieb, L. (1991). Marital intimacy in bereaved and nonbereaved couples: A comparative study. In D. Papadatou & C. Papadatou (Eds.), *Children and death.* pp. 267–275. New York: Hemisphere Publishing.

Lansky, S. B., Cairns, N. V., Hassanein, M. R., Wehr, J., & Lowman, J. T. (1978). Childhood cancer: Parental discord and divorce. *Pediatrics, 62,* 184–188.

Latour, K. (1983). *For those who live: Helping children cope with the death of a brother or sister.* Dallas, TX: Kathy Latour.

Lazarus, R. S., & Cohen, J. B. (1977). Environmental stress. In I. Attman & J. F. Wohlwill (Eds.), *Human behavior and environment (Vol.2).* New York: Plenum Press.

Leenaars, A. A. (1991). *Life span perspectives of suicide.* New York: Plenum Press.

Lefley, H. P. (1992). The stigmatized family. In P. J. Fingk & A. Tasman (Eds)., *Stigma and mental illness.* pp. 127–138. Washington, DC: American Psychiatric Press.

Lehman, D. R., Ellard, J. H., & Wortman, C. B. (1985). Social support for the bereaved: Recipients' and providers' perspectives on what is helpful. *Journal of Consulting and Clinical Psychology, 20,* 2–30.

Lieberman, M. A., Mennaghan, A., & Mullan, J. T. (1981). The stress process. *Journal of Health and Social Behavior, 22,* 337–356.

Lietar, E. F. (1986). Miscarriage. In T. A. Rando (Ed.), *Parental loss of a child.* pp. 121–128. Champaign, IL: Research Press.

Lin, N., Simone, R. S., & Ensel, W. M. (1979). Social support, stressful events, and illness: A model and an empirical test. *Journal of Health and Social Behavior, 20,* 108–119.

Lindemann, E. (1944). Symptomatology and management of acute grief. *American Journal of Psychiatry, 101,* 141–149.

Lord, J. H. (1987). Survivor grief following a drunk-driving crash. *Death Studies, 11,* 413–435.

Lorenz, K. (1963). *On aggression.* London: Methuen.

Lund, D. A. (Ed.). (1989). *Older bereaved spouses: Research with practical applications.* New York: Hemisphere Publishing.

Lund, D. A., Caserta, M. S., & Dimond, M. F. (1989). Impact of spousal bereavement on the subjective well-being of older adults. In D. A. Lund (Ed.), *Older bereaved spouses: Research with practical applications.* pp. 3–16. New York: Hemisphere Publishing.

Lundin, T. (1984). Morbidity following sudden and unexpected bereavement. *British Journal of Psychiatry, 145,* 424–428.

Mahoney, M. J. (1991). *Human change processes: Scientific foundations of psychotherapy.* New York: Basic Books.

Maier, S. F., & Seligman, M. E. P. (1976). Learned helplessness: Theory and evidence. *Journal of Experimental Psychiatry. General, 105,* 3–46.

Martin, J. L. (1988). Psychological consequences of AIDS-related bereavement among gay men. *Journal of Consulting and Clinical Psychology, 56,* 856–862.

Martinson, I. A. (1991). Grief is an individual journey: Follow-up of families' postdeath of a child with cancer. In D. Papadatou & C. Papadatou (Eds.), *Children and death.* pp. 255–265. New York: Hemisphere Publishing.

Maslow, A. H. (1968). *Toward psychology of being.* New York: Van Nostrand.

Mawson, D., Marks, I., Ramm, L., & Stern, R. (1981). Guided mourning for morbid grief: A controlled study. *British Journal of Psychiatry, 138,* 185–193.

McIntosh, J. L. (1987). Survivor family relationships: Literature review. In E. J. Dunne, J. L. McIntosh, & K. DunneMaxin (Eds.), *Suicide and its aftermath.* pp. 73–84. New York: W. W. Norton.

McIntosh, J. L. (1991). Epidemiology of suicide in the U.S. In A. A. Leenaars, *Life span perspectives of suicide.* pp. 55–70. New York: Plenum Press.

McMann, I. L., & Pearlman, L. A. (1990). Vicarious traumatization: A framework for understanding the psychological effects of working with victims. *Journal of Traumatic Stress Studies, 3*(1), 131–149.

Merriam-Webster, Inc. (1976). *Webster's Collegiate Thesaurus.* Springfield, MA: Merriam-Webster, Inc.

Miles, M. S., & Crandell, E. K. R. (1983). The search for meaning and its potential for affecting growth in bereaved parents. *Health Values: Achieving High Level Wellness, 7*(1), 19–23.

Miles, M. S., & Demi, A. S. (1983-84). Toward the development of a theory of bereavement: Sources of guilt in bereaved parents. *Omega, 14*(3), 299–314.

Moss, M. S., & Moss, S. Z. (1983-84). The impact of parental death on middle-aged children. *Omega, 14*(1), 65–75.

National Highway Traffic Safety Administration. (1992, July). Fatal Accident Reporting System.

Ness, D. E., & Pfeffer, C. (1990). Sequelae of bereavement resulting from suicide. *American Journal of Psychiatry, 147*(3), 279–285.

Nichols, J. (1986, November). Illegitimate mourners. In *Children and death: Perspectives and challenges.* Symposium sponsored by Children's Hospital Medical Center of Akron, Akron, OH.

Norris, F. H., & Murrell, S. A. (1988). Prior experience as a moderator of disaster impact on anxiety symptoms in older adults. *American Journal of Community Psychology, 16,* 664–683.

Novello, A. C. (1991). Women and HIV infection. *Journal of the American Medical Association, 265,* 1805.

Ochberg, F. M. (1988). *Post-traumatic therapy and victims of violence.* New York: Brunner/Mazel.

Osterweis, M., Solomon, F., & Green, M. (Eds.). (1984). *Bereavement: Reactions, consequences and care.* Report by the Committee for the Study of Health Consequences of the Stress of Bereavement, Institute of Medicine, National Academy of Sciences. Washington, DC: National Academy Press.

Owen, G., Fulton, R., & Markusen, E. (1982). Death at a distance: A study of family survivors. *Omega, 13*(3), 191–225.

Page, R. (1984). *Stigma.* London: Routledge & Kegan Paul.

Parkes, C. M. (1975). Determinants of outcome following bereavements. *Omega, 6,* 303–323.

Parkes, C. M., & Brown, R. (1972). Health after bereavement: A controlled study of young Boston widows and widowers. *Psychosomatic Medicine, 34,* 449–461.

Parkes, C. M., & Weiss, R. S. (1983). *Recovery from bereavement.* New York: Basic Books.

Pavlov, I. P. (1927). *Conditioned reflexes: An investigation of the physiological activity of the cerebral cortex.* New York: Dover, Anrep GV.

Pedhauzur, E. J. (1982). *Multiple regression in behavioral research: Explanation and prediction.* New York: Holt, Rinehart & Winston.

Peppers, L. C., & Knapp, R. J. (1980). *Motherhood and mourning.* New York: Praeger.

Pfeffer, C. (1986). *The suicidal child.* New York: Guilford Press.

Phifer, J. F., & Norris, F. H. (1989). Psychological symptoms in older adults following natural disaster: Nature, timing, duration and course. *Journal of Gerontology: Social Sciences, 44,* S206–S217.

Poussaint, A. F. (1984). *The grief response following a homicide.* Paper presented at the annual meeting of the American Psychological Association, August, Toronto, Canada.

Pynoos, R., & Spencer, F. (1985). *Interaction of trauma and grief in childhood.* pp.1–13. Washington, DC: American Psychiatric Press.

Rando, T. A. (1984). *Grief, dying and death: Criminal interventions for caregivers.* Champaign, IL: Research Press.

Rando, T. A. (1986a). A comprehensive analysis of anticipatory grief: Perspective, processes, and problems. In T. A. Rando (Ed.), *Loss of anticipatory grief.* pp. 3–38. Lexington, MA: Lexington Books.

Rando, T. A. (1986b). *Parental loss of a child.* Champaign, IL: Research Press.

Rando, T. A. (1993). *Treatment of complicated mourning*. Champaign, IL: Research Press.

Raphael, B. (1977). Preventive intervention with the recently bereaved. *Archives of General Psychiatry, 34*, 1450–1454.

Raphael, B. (1984). *The anatomy of bereavement*. London: Hutchinson Publishing.

Riley, J. L., & Green, R. R. (1993). Influence of education on self-perceived attitudes about HIV/AIDS among human service providers. *Social Work, 38*(4), 396–401.

Rinear, E. (1984). *Parental response to child murder: An exploratory study*. Unpublished doctoral dissertation., University of Michigan, Ann Arbor.

Rosen, E. J. (1990). *Families facing death*. Lexington, MA: Lexington Books.

Rosenberg, G. (1989). *The future of medical crisis counseling: Services for the chronically ill, their families, and significant others*. Baltimore, MD: School of Social Work, University of Maryland at Baltimore.

Sanders, C. M. (1986). Accidental death of a child. In T. A. Rando (Ed.), *Parental loss of a child*. pp. 181–190. Champaign, IL: Research Press.

Sanders, C. M. (1989). *Grief: The mourning after*. New York: John Wiley & Sons.

Scarr, S. (1982). Development is internally guided, not determined. *Contemporary Psychology, 27*, 852–853.

Schiff, H. S. (1977). *The bereaved parent*. New York: Crown Publishers.

Schmidt, G., & Weiner, B. (1988). An attribution-affect-action theory of behavior: Replications of judgments of help-giving. *Personality and Social Psychology Bulletin, 14*, 610–621.

Schuster, T. L., & Butler, E. W. (1989). Bereavement, social networks, social support, and mental health. In D. A. Lund (Ed.), *Older bereaved spouses: Research with practical applications*. pp. 55–68. New York: Hemisphere Publishing.

Seligman, M. E. P., & Maier, S. R. (1968). Failure to escape traumatic shock. *Journal of Experimental Psychology, 74*(1), 1–9.

Shaver, K. G. (1985). *The attributions of blame: Causality, responsibility and blameworthiness*. New York: Springer-Verlag.

Shore, J. H., Tatum, E. L., & Volmer, W. M. (1986). Psychiatric reactions to disaster: The Mount St. Helens experience. *American Journal of Psychiatry, 143*, 590–595.

Sigelman, C. K., Howell, J. L., Cornell, D. P., Cutright, J. D., & Dewey, J. C. (1991). Courtesy stigma: The social implication of associating with a gay person. *Journal of Social Psychology, 131*(1), 45–56.

Silver, R. L., & Wortman, C. B. (1980). Coping with undesirable life events. In J. Garber & M. E. P. Seligman (Eds.), *Human helplessness: Theory and applications*. pp. 279–375. New York: Basic Books.

Silverman, P. R. (1970). The widow as a caregiver in a program of preventive intervention with other widows. *Mental Hygiene, 54*, 540–547.

Simpson, M. A. (1979). *The facts of death*. Englewood Cliffs, NJ: Prentice-Hall.

Singleton, G., & Teahan, J. (1978). Effects of job-related stress on the physical and psychological adjustment of police officers. *Journal of Police Science and Administration, 6*, 13–18.

Sinick, D. (1977). *Counseling older persons careers, retirement, dying*. New York: Human Sciences Press.

Solomon, S. D., Smith, E. M., Robins, L. N., & Fischbach, R. L. (1987). Social involvement as a mediator of disaster-induced stress. *Journal of Applied Social Psychology, 17,* 1092–1112.

Spitzer, R. L., & Williams, J. B. (1985). *Structured clinical interview for DSM-II-R, patient version.* New York: State Psychiatric Institute, Biometrics Research Department.

Sprang, M. V. (1991). *Factors influencing the extent of mourning, the extent of grieving and post-traumatic stress disorder symptomatology in surviving family members after a drunk driving facility.* Unpublished doctoral dissertation, University of Texas at Arlington, Arlington, TX.

Sprang, M. V., McNeil, J. S., & Wright, R. (1989, March). The psychological changes after the murder of a significant other. *Social Casework, 70*(3), 159–162.

Sprang, M. V., McNeil, J. S., & Wright, R. (1993). Grief among surviving family members of homicide victims: A causal approach. *Omega, 26*(2), 145–160.

Steinglass, P., & Gerrity, E. (1990). Natural disasters and post-traumatic stress disorder: Short-term versus long-term recovery in two disaster-affected communities. *Journal of Applied Social Psychology, 20,* 1746–1765.

Stephens, S. (1972). *Death comes home.* New York: Morehouse-Barlow.

Stillion, J. M., McDowell, E. E., & May, J. H. (1989). *Suicide across the life span— premature exits.* New York: Hemisphere Publishing.

Strauss, A. (1975). *Chronic illness and the quality of life.* St. Louis, MO: Mosby.

Stroebe, W., & Stroebe, M. S. (1987). *Bereavement and health: The psychological consequences of partner loss.* New York: Cambridge University Press.

Terr, L. C. (1983). Chowchilla revisited: The effects of psychic trauma 4 years after a school bus kidnapping. *American Journal of Psychiatry, 140*(12), 1543–1550.

Thompson, J. G. (1988). *The psychobiology of emotions.* New York: Plenum Press.

Thompson, L., Breckenridge, J., Gallegher, D., & Peterson, J. (1984). Effects of bereavement on self-perceptions of physical health in elderly widows and widowers. *Journal of Gerontology, 39,* 309–314.

Titchener, J. L., & Kapp, F. T. (1976). Family and character change at Buffalo Creek. *American Journal of Psychiatry, 133,* 295–299.

Trice, A. D. (1988). Posttraumatic stress syndrome-like symptoms among AIDS caregivers. *Psychological Reports, 63,* 656–658.

Turner, R. J., Frankel, G., & Levin, D. M. (1983). Social support: conceptualization, measurement, and implications for mental health. *Research in Community Mental Health, 3,* 67–111.

U.S. Bureau of Census. (1987). *Statistical abstract of the U.S.* (197th ed.). Washington, DC: U.S. Government Printing Office.

Vachon, M. L. S., Sheldon, A. R., Lancee, W. J., Lyall, W. A. L., Rogers, J., & Freeman, S. J. J. (1980). Controlled study of self-help intervention for widows. *American Journal of Psychiatry, 137,* 1380–1384.

Viney, L. Z., Henry, R. M., Walker, B. M., & Crooks, L. (1992). The psychosocial impact of multiple deaths from AIDS. *Omega, 24*(2), 151–153.

Vital statistics of the United States. (1993). Hyattsville, MD: U.S. Department of Health and Human Services, Public Health Service, CDC.

Volkan, V. (1975). "Re-grief" therapy. In B. Schoenberg, I. Gerber, A. Wiener, A. H. Kutscher, D. Peretz, & A. C. Carr (Eds.), *Bereavement: Its psychosocial aspects.* New York: Columbia University Press.

Walster, E., Walster, G. W., & Berscheid, E. (1978). *Equity: Theory and research.* Boston, MA: Allyn & Bacon.

Weinbach, R. W. (1989). Sudden death and secret survivors: Helping those who grieve alone. *Social Work, 34*(1), 57–60.

Westberg, G. E. (1971). *Good grief.* Philadelphia: Fortress Press.

Wilkinson, C. B. (1983). Aftermath of disaster, collapse of the Hyatt Regency skywalk. *American Journal of Psychiatry, 140,* 1134–1139.

Wilson, J. P. (1980). *Towards an understanding of post-traumatic stress disorder among Vietnam veterans.* Testimony before U.S. Senate Subcommittee on Veteran Affairs, May.

Wolfelt, A. D. (1988). *Death and grief: A guide for the clergy.* Muncie, IN: Accelerated Development.

Worden, J. W. (1982). *Grief counseling and grief therapy: A handbook for the mental health practitioner.* New York: Springer.

Wuthrow, R., Christiano, K., & Kuzlowski, J. (1980). Religion and bereavement: A conceptual framework. *Journal of the Scientific Study of Religion, 19,* 408–422.

Zisook, S., & Devaul, R. (1984). Measuring acute grief. *Psychiatric Medicine, 2*(2), 169–175.

Zisook, S., Devaul, R. A., & Click Jr., M. A. (1982). Measuring symptoms of grief and bereavement. *American Journal of Psychiatry, 139,* 1590–1592.

Name Index

Subject Index